CREATIVE
Wedding
Decorations
YOU CAN MAKE

EDITED BY TERESA NELSON

BETTERWAY BOOKS
CINCINNATI, OHIO

Thanks to the following people who designed the projects in this book.
LeNae Gerig
Janet Immordino
Julianna Manier
Judith Meredith
Teresa Nelson
Rich Salvaggio, aaf, AIFD
Kathy Thompson

Creative Wedding Decorations You Can Make. Copyright © 1998 by Hot off the Press. Manufactured in the United States of America. All rights reserved. No part of this book may be reproduced in any form or by any electronic or mechanical means including information storage and retrieval systems without permission in writing from the publisher, except by a reviewer, who may quote brief passages in a review. Published by Betterway Books, an imprint of F&W Publications, Inc., 1507 Dana Avenue, Cincinnati, Ohio 45207. (800) 289-0963. First edition.

Other fine Betterway Books are available from your local bookstore or direct from the publisher.

02   01   00   99   5   4   3

Library of Congress Cataloging-in-Publication Data

Creative wedding decorations you can make/edited by Teresa Nelson.
   p.   cm.
ISBN 1-55870-484-1 (pbk. : alk. paper)
   1. Handicraft..   2. Wedding decorations.   3. Bridal bouquets.
4. Flower arrangement.   I. Nelson, Teresa.
TT149.C74 1998   97-49012
745.594'1—dc21   CIP

Edited by Teresa Nelson
Content Edited by David Borcherding
Production Edited by Michelle Kramer
Interior art production by Kathleen DeZarn

Table of Contents

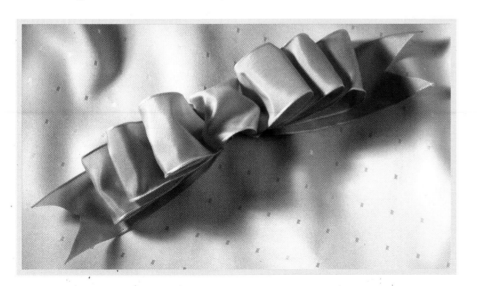

General Instructions

BASIC FLORAL SUPPLIES:

When you do florals, in addition to the materials listed for each project, you will want:

- scissors
- measuring tape
- heavy-duty wire cutters
- low-temperature glue gun and sticks
- tacky craft glue
- 22- and 30-gauge wire
- floral tape (white or green)
- 2½" (6.4cm) wired wood floral picks
- wastebasket

FLOWER MEASUREMENTS

When a length is given, measure from the flower tip to the stem end.

When a blossom length is given, measure only the blossom.

When a stem length is given, measure only the stem.

When a blossom width is given, measure the open flower face.

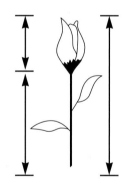

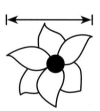

STEMS & SPRIGS

A "stem" refers to an entire stem of flowers as purchased. When cut apart, the individual pieces become "sprigs" to be inserted into a design.

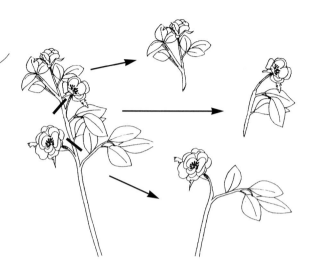

BASIC BOUQUET HOLDER

Many of the projects in this book call for a bouquet holder with a collar. The holder has a cylinder of foam in a plastic cage attached to a handle. The collar slides up the handle and locks into place below the cage. Its tulle ruffle covers the foam and stem ends from the back.

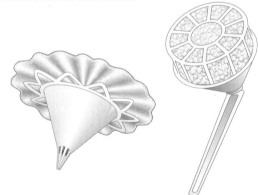

General Instructions

Floral Taping:
White ½" (1.3cm) wide floral tape was used throughout this book. Floral tape does not have a right or wrong side, it's not a sticky tape and it will only become tacky and adhere to itself when stretched.

Wrap the tape around the base of the two items to be secured together and squeeze the ends together to adhere. Holding the tape with your right hand, stretch it and pull, angling downward.

Twist the stem with the thumb and forefinger of your left hand. As you are twisting, the tape should be covering the stem snugly, overlapping its way down the stem. At the bottom, break the tape off and press the ends together.

In some places on the headpieces, you won't be able to freely twist the stems, so you'll need to break off the tape in 6"-8" (15.2cm-20.3cm) lengths. Again, pinch the ends of the tape together to begin, and then wrap the tape around and through the pieces.

Coloring Floral Pieces:
Colored floral pieces are appropriate for bridesmaids and second-time brides. If you are unable to find pieces in the desired colors, spray white pieces with fabric or floral dye. Design Master brand colors are excellent. Acrylic spray paints are not recommended because they leave flowers stiff to the touch and may spot them.

Attaching Combs:
Combs can be hand sewn to headpieces and veils for added security. Using a long whipstitch, sew combs to the gathered edge of any veil after the veil has been hand sewn to the headpiece.

When no veil is used, sew the comb to the headpiece where it meets the head. Using strong thread, stitch around and through the comb and the stems of the headpiece.

For extra strength, apply hot glue or tacky glue between the comb and headpiece; allow to dry overnight.

Hairpin Hooks:
Used in conjunction with combs or on their own, hairpin hooks allow the headpiece to be securely pinned into the hair.

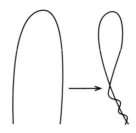

To form, bend a 4" (10.2cm) piece of white cloth-covered wire into a loop and twist the ends once or twice. Place this loop on the headpiece, add a small amount of hot or tacky glue to hold and use floral tape to cover the wire ends.

It is best to use at least three hairpin hooks per headpiece, one on each end of the headpiece and one centrally located.

Satin Wrap:
Use ¼"-½" (.6cm-1.3cm) wide satin ribbon to wrap around the headpiece stems before adding a veil (or even when a veil will not be used) to finish off the headpiece. Begin by gluing down one end of the ribbon, then wrap completely and securely, and glue down the other end. Trim away excess ribbon.

PREPARATION OF CHARMS

Antiquing:
Use a cotton swab to apply black acrylic paint to the charm, completely covering the front. Before it dries, wipe with a paper towel to remove some paint—you control how much. Let the charm dry.

Sealing:
All charms should be sealed, since they are brass and will darken with time. Spray with a gloss varnish; let dry. Turn them over and spray the backs; let dry.

MITERING CORNERS

Fold one side over the edge and glue—continue gluing past the corner, gluing the fabric to itself. The glued area will remain straight when you fold that side over the other edge.

General Instructions —Veils

TYPES & CONSTRUCTION OF VEILS

There are four types of veils used in this book:

- *Type 1*—Needed: 45" (114.3cm) length of 54" (137.2cm) wide tulle. Round the corners. Fold the tulle to form a 20" (50.8cm) and 25" (63.5cm) layer. Sew a running stitch at the fold and gather to the width indicated in the project instructions.

- *Type 2*—Needed: 45" (114.3cm) length of 54" (137.2cm) wide tulle. Round the corners. Fold to form a 20" (50.8cm) and 25" (63.5cm) layer. Sew a running stitch along the center 10" (25.4cm) of the fold and gather to 3"(7.6cm).

- *Type 3*—Needed: 1 yard (91.4cm) of 108" (274.3cm) wide tulle. Round the corners. Sew a running stitch along one 108" (274.3cm) edge and gather to the width indicated in the project instructions.

- *Type 4*—Needed: 55" (139.7cm) length of 108" (274.3cm) wide tulle. Round the corners. Fold the tulle to form a 23" (58.4cm) and 32" (81.3cm) layer. Sew a running stitch at the fold and gather to the width indicated in the project instructions.

HINTS FOR HANDLING TULLE

The tulle in this book is available in craft and fabric stores. Use the 108" (274cm) wide tulle, and cut it in half for most projects. If static is a problem, especially on a dry winter day, keep a spray bottle filled with water handy. Give the tulle a spritz if it starts to get unruly. It is a good idea to iron out any wrinkles after you've cut the tulle; use a low setting or the material may melt. Some projects use loops for securing the projects to the head with hairpins. However, the loops are optional in all the projects.

VEIL LENGTHS

There are five basic lengths:

- *Shoulder length*—20" (50.8cm). Typically combined with other lengths for a double-layer veil.

- *Elbow length*—36" (91.4cm). This veil is used with short or informal gowns.

- *Fingertip length*—45" (114.3cm). For semiformal and formal weddings.

- *Chapel length*—72" (182.9cm). This veil reaches just to the floor and is used in semiformal and formal weddings.

- *Cathedral length*—96" (244cm). This veil is for formal weddings and formal gowns with cathedral trains.

These lengths can be combined for a double-layer veil. Add the lengths together to determine where to cut the tulle, then fold it for the layers and sew a running stitch at the fold. Pull to gather, then attach to the headpiece.

Shoulder

Elbow

Fingertip

Chapel

BRIDAL VEIL CONSTRUCTION

Single Layer Veil:
Veil: Tulle may be 54" (137.2cm) or 108" (274cm) wide, according to the desired fullness. Use the guideline on page 8 to determine the length.

1. Fold the tulle in half as shown in the diagram below.
2. Use sharp scissors to cut a curve as indicated by the shaded area.
3. Unfold the tulle and hand sew a gathering stitch 1" (2.5cm) from the edge along the top. After adding any desired trim, pull the threads, gathering the veil to fit the hat or headpiece. Glue or stitch to the headpiece.

To make multiple veil layers: Place the lengths together, matching the top edges. Baste the layers together then gather as in step 3.

Pouf Veil:
Add 18" or 24" to the length given for any veil. Use 24" to create a fuller pouf and 18" for a smaller pouf.

1. Follow steps 1 and 2 of the single layer veil directions given above.
2. Unfold the tulle, then refold the top portion (see below) to create a 9" (22.9cm) or 12" (30.5cm) pouf.
3. Hand sew a gathering stitch across the top of the veil, catching all three layers. After adding any desired trim, pull the threads and gather the veil to fit the hat or headpiece. Glue or stitch to the headpiece.

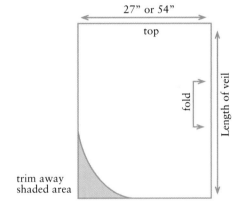

27" or 54"

top

fold

Length of veil

trim away
shaded area

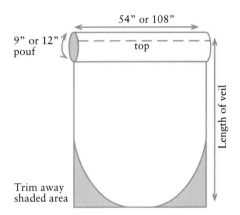

54" or 108"

9" or 12"
pouf

top

Length of veil

Trim away
shaded area

General Instructions—Headpieces

HEADPIECES

Selecting a Headpiece:
The style of the wedding dress is an important consideration when choosing a headpiece. If the gown is heavily beaded, the headpiece should carry the same feeling. If the gown has iridescent touches, so should the headpiece. Other factors to consider are height, hairstyle and the shape of the face. Five headpiece styles are described here.

Floral Clusters:
Stems of flowers are floral taped together to make a cluster. Ready-made clusters are available, or one can be created. If designed to have a veil, the cluster is worn toward the back of the head and can be very effective with long or upswept hair.

Without a veil, the cluster can be pinned just above the ear with hair swept back from the side of the face. The cluster is an excellent style for bridesmaids or second-time brides.

Wreaths:
This headpiece, a floral band, may be interwoven with ribbons, pearls, tulle and other materials. The wreath can circle the forehead or the crown of the head, depending on its size. When formed small enough, a wreath can make a lovely communion veil.

This book includes instructions for creating wreaths or trimming ready-made wreaths. Smaller ready-made wreaths can be enlarged by cutting two wreaths apart and floral taping them together to make one long piece. Overlap the ends 2"–3" (5.1cm-7.6cm), form a circle, then twist the wire ends together and secure with floral tape. Attach a veil or bow at this spot.

Bands:

The band is centered on top of the head and is most effective on rounded faces or hairstyles with bangs. A cascade can be added to one or both sides of the band to work well with longer hair.

For a full look, use flowers and pearls. If less height is desired, use appliqués and lace in place of the florals.

Sidesweeps:
Appropriately named, this style curves along the side of the face and extends partly over the top of the head, forming a crescent. If desired, the effect can be lengthened with a cascade.

This headpiece works well when the hair is pulled back from that side of the face, adding to the upswept look.

Hats and Caps:
The hat can be worn with or without a veil. A hat with a wide brim is appropriate for a semiformal or garden wedding and accents shoulder-length hair. A narrower brim is more formal and can be elaborately trimmed, with one side wired to the crown if desired.

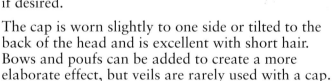

The cap is worn slightly to one side or tilted to the back of the head and is excellent with short hair. Bows and poufs can be added to create a more elaborate effect, but veils are rarely used with a cap.

General Instructions—Ribbons & Bows

The ribbons you use can determine the entire look of your design. For example, heavy tapestries give a more European look; narrow satin ribbons add a light, romantic effect. The ribbon should tie the design together and actually become part of it.

In choosing a ribbon, both color and width play important roles. Incompatible colors or textures can produce a jarring effect. Using a ribbon that has all the colors in the design--or nearly all of them--ties the design together.

If one ribbon with the right colors can't be found, use two or three ribbons, each in one of the colors needed, and stack the bows. Make a large bow of the widest ribbon (usually the dominant color in the design), and then wire or glue a smaller bow of narrower ribbon to the center of it.

Another method of tying colors together is to make one bow of several different ribbons. Hold them together and handle them as if they were one length to make a bow of the desired size and type.

How Much Do I Need?

Although projects in this book include the yardage needed for each bow in the materials list, you may want to make a different bow. First decide how many loops and tails you want and how long they will be (if you want a center loop, double its length, add ½" [1.3cm] and add this measurement along with the tails). Then do this easy math:

1. ___" (loop length) x 2 + ½" (1.3cm) extra (for the twist) = **A**

2. **A** x (number of loops) = **B**

3. **B** +___" (tail length) +___" (tail length) = **C**

4. **C** ÷ 36" (91.4cm) = yardage required.

For Example:
To make a bow with eight 4" (10.2cm) loops, a 6" (15.2cm) tail and a 7" (17.8cm) tail

1. 4" (10.2cm) x 2 + ½" (1.3cm) = **8½"** (21.6cm)

2. 8½" (21.6cm) x 8 loops = **68"** (172.7cm)

3. **68"** (172.7cm) + 6" (15.2cm) (tail length) + 7" (17.8cm) (tail length) = **81"** (205.7cm)

4. **81"** (205.7cm) ÷ 36" (91.4cm) = 2.25 or 2¼ yards (205.65cm).

RIBBON WIDTHS

#40   *about 2⅞" (7.3cm)*

#16   *about 2" (5.1cm)*

#9   *about 1½" (3.8cm)*

#5   *about ⅞" (2.2cm)*

#3   *about ⅝" (1.6cm)*

#2   *about ½" (1.2cm)*

#1 ½   *about ⅜" (1cm)*

#1   *about ¼" (.6cm)*

Many times ribbon is used to bring different design elements together visually. This is done by tucking, rippling or looping ribbon lengths or the bow tails among the other materials in the project. Twisting the ribbon as it's looped adds interest.

Other materials such as pearls, beads or cord can be used with or in place of ribbon.

For wide ribbons, a couched effect can be achieved by pinching the ribbon every few inches and wrapping the pinched areas with 30-gauge wire. The ribbon will puff between the wires. Glue the wired areas into the design.

Bouquets

Spring Bouquet
Autumn Bridal Bouquet
Peaches & Cream Pomander Bouquet
Attendant Spring Basket
Burgundy Rose Bouquet
Pink Modified Waterfall
Purple Mound Bouquet
Purple Hand-Tied Bouquet
Coral Crescent Bouquet
Bride's Cascade Bouquet
Maid's Mound Bouquet
Flower Girl's
Hair Clip & Basket
Maid's Orchid Bouquet
Rose And Alstroemeria Bouquet
Garden Rites Bride's Bouquet
Garden Rites Maid's Bouquet
Spider Plant Bouquet
Orchid And Smilax Bouquet
Candlelight Bride's Bouquet
Tosser Bouquet

SPRING BOUQUET

two stems of white silk peonies,
each with one 4" (10.2cm) wide blossom
and one 2" (5.1cm) long bud

two 21" (53.3cm) stems of white silk lilacs, each with
five 2"–5" (5.1cm-12.7cm) long blossom heads

two 22" (55.9cm) stems of cream silk mini rosebuds,
each with seven 1" (2.5cm) long buds

two 24" (61cm) stems of white silk stocks,
each with two 5" (12.7cm) blossom spires

three 26" (66cm) stems of white silk tulips,
each with one 3" (7.6cm) wide blossom

three 23" (58.4cm) stems of white silk rosebuds,
each with one 2" (5.1cm) long bud

one green silk ruffled-leaf ivy bush
with four 12"–24" (30.5cm-61cm) branches
of 3 1/4"–2" (1.9cm-5.1cm) wide leaves

five 12"–20" (30.5cm-50.8cm) stems of preserved
green plumosus fern

4 yards (365.8cm) of 3 1/2" (8.9cm) wide
sheer platinum wire-edged ribbon

basic supplies (see page 6)

1. Cut the peonies to 17" (43.2cm) and 21" (53.3cm). Hold with your hand 8" (20.3cm) above the stem ends, with the 17" (43.2cm) blossom on the left. Cut the lilac stems to 21" (53.3cm) and hold one on each side of the peonies, shaping the blossom heads to curve out and down.

2. Cut the mini-rosebud stems to 22" (55.9cm). Position one in front of and one behind the left peony. Cut the stock stems to 24" (61cm). Position one in front of and one behind the right peony.

3. Cut each tulip to 26" (66cm) and each rosebud to 23" (58.4cm); insert them between the peonies. Curve the tulips right; curve the rosebuds slightly left. Trim the leaves from the lowest 8" (20.3cm) of each stem. Cut the branches from the ivy bush, and cut the longest one in half. Place evenly spaced around the bottom of the flowers as shown.

4. Insert the fern stems to fill empty spaces between the flowers. Wrap wire securely around the stems just below the lowest leaves. Use the ribbon to make a puffy bow with eight 6" (15.2cm) loops and 18" (45.7cm) tails. Glue at the left of the wire. Wrap one tail to cover the wire and the bow center, gluing to secure. Ripple the tails down the right side of the stems. Cut the stems even 8" (20.3cm) below the bow.

Note:
A matching attendant basket is on page 17.

AUTUMN BRIDAL BOUQUET

A U T U M N
B R I D A L   B O U Q U E T

one green silk ivy bush with five 6" (15.2cm) and
five 16" (40.6cm) branches of
1"–3" (2.5cm–7.6cm) wide leaves

one 3" (7.6cm) Styrofoam bouquet holder
with an 8" (20.3cm) white bouquet collar

three 4" (10.2cm) wide maroon silk roses

2 yards (182.9cm) of 3 ½" (8.9cm)
purple/gold sheer wire-edged ribbon

two 12" (30.5cm) pyracantha stems, each with a
6" (15.2cm) long cluster of ¼" (.6cm) green berries

three 1" (2.5cm) long maroon silk rosebuds

two 3" (7.6cm) wide maroon silk opening roses

two 2" (5.1cm) long maroon silk rosebuds

four 4" (10.2cm) wide dried green hydrangea heads
with 6" (15.2cm) stems

three stems of dried yellow yarrow

four 12"–20" (30.5cm–50.8cm) twigs of honeysuckle
or grapevine

basic supplies (see page 6)

1. Cut the 16" (40.6cm) ivy branches from the bush. Insert into the foam sides at the 5:00, 6:00, 9:00, 10:00 and 12:00 positions. Cut two open roses with 6" (15.2cm) stems and insert in the foam center, with one extending forward and the other at 11:00. Cut the last open rose with an 8" (20.3cm) stem and insert it in the center at 12:00.

2. Use the ribbon to make a puffy bow with two 6" (15.2cm) loops and 18" (45.7cm) tails. Wire to a wood pick and insert at the lower left edge. Insert the pyracantha stems at the bow center, one curving up and the other curving to the right. Cut the small rosebuds to 10" (25.4cm), 12" (30.5cm) and 16" (40.6cm). Insert the 10" (25.4cm) stem above the bow center, the 12" (30.5cm) stem below the center rose and the 16" (40.6cm) stem into the foam lower right. Curve each stem so the bud faces forward.

3. Cut one opening rose to 5" (12.7cm) and insert at the center right. Cut the other to 8" (20.3cm) and insert at the bottom, curving down and right. Cut a large rosebud to 9" (22.9cm) and insert just above the 5" (12.7cm) rose; cut the other bud to 10" (25.4cm) and insert just right of the 8" (20.3cm) rose.

4. Insert hydrangea heads above, right and left of the lowest open rose. Insert the last head at the far left side. Insert the yarrow stems above the highest hydrangea. Cut the 6" (15.2cm) ivy stems from the bush and insert around the bouquet edges, covering any exposed foam. Insert the vines evenly spaced among the open roses.

PEACHES & CREAM POMANDER BOUQUET

P E A C H E S   &   C R E A M
P O M A N D E R   B O U Q U E T

½ yard (45.7cm) of 3½" (8.9cm) wide peach sheer wire-edged ribbon

one 3" (7.6cm) Styrofoam ball

three peach silk rose stems, each with one 4" (10.2cm) wide blossom

three white silk rosebud stems, each with a 2" (5.1cm) bud

three peach silk rosebud stems, each with a 2" (5.1cm) bud

one stem of white silk hydrangea with a 5" (12.7cm) wide blossom head

two stems of peach silk statice, each with three 2½" (6.4cm) blossom heads

one stem of peach silk trailing wild rose, with three 1½"–3" (3.8cm–7.6cm) blossoms, a 1" (2.5cm) opening bud and two ½" (1.3cm) buds

one green silk ivy bush, with six 6" (15.2cm) branches of ¾"–1¾" (1.9cm–4.5cm) leaves

three stems of green preserved plumosus fern

ten 8"–12" (20.3cm–30.5cm) twigs of honeysuckle or grapevine

one U-shaped floral pin

basic supplies (see page 6)

1. Hold the ribbon ends together and U-pin to the top of the ball for a handle. Cut each rose and rosebud with a 3" (7.6cm) stem. Insert one rose into the center front of the ball. Insert the others low toward the back, one on each side. Insert a peach bud low in the front and one above each side rose. Insert the white buds, evenly spaced, around the front rose.

2. Cut the florets of the hydrangea head into five bunches. Wire each bunch to a wood pick. Insert one bunch between each pair of rosebuds, and the last two high and low on the back of the ball.

3. Cut each statice head to 6" (15.2cm) and each wild rose with a 3" (7.6cm) stem. Cut the 6" (15.2cm) branches from the ivy bush. Insert, evenly spaced, among the flowers.

4. Cut the remaining rose leaf sprigs from the stems. Insert to fill empty spaces, covering all the foam. Cut the fern to 8"–12" (20.3cm–30.5cm) sprigs and glue, evenly spaced, around the ball. Insert the vines, evenly spaced, around the ball, curving to follow the shape of the arrangement as shown above.

ATTENDANT SPRING BASKET

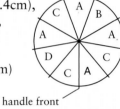

ATTENDANT SPRING BASKET

three stems of pink silk freesia,
each with three 4" (10.2cm) long blossom sprays

three stems of peach silk statice,
each with four 3" (7.6cm) blossom clusters
on three 10"–12" (25.4cm–30.5cm) sprigs

four stems of blue silk stock,
each with two 5" (12.7cm) long blossom spires

four stems of white silk lilacs,
each with five 4" (10.2cm) wide blossom heads

3 ounces (85.1g) preserved green plumosus fern

one 4" x 11" (10.2cm x 27.9cm) round white wicker
basket with a 7" (17.8cm) tall handle

3½ yards (320cm) of 3" (7.6cm) wide
light coral sheer ribbon

basic supplies (see page 6)

1. Cut each freesia spray to 10" (25.4cm), each statice cluster to 10" (25.4cm), each stock spire to 8" (20.3cm) and each lilac head to 7" (17.8cm). Cut three dozen 7"–10" (17.8cm–25.4cm) plumosus sprigs. Make bundles as follows:

handle front

A. (make 4): 1 freesia, 1 statice, 1 stock, 2 lilac, 4 fern
B. (make 1): 1 freesia, 1 statice, 1 stock, 3 lilac, 4 fern
C. (make 3): 1 freesia, 2 statice, 1 stock, 2 lilac, 4 fern
D. (make 1): 1 freesia, 1 statice, 3 lilac, 4 fern

Hold the elements of each bundle with the stem ends even and wrap securely with floral wire 2" (5.1cm) from the ends.

2. Place the basket with one handle end near you and glue the bundles along the basket rim as diagrammed above. Each bundle should extend clockwise, with its stems covered by the next bundle's blossoms. Insert 6"–8" (15.2cm–20.3cm) wire lengths through the basket weave to help secure the bundles. Trim the excess wire.

3. Cut the lilac leaves from the stems in sprigs of two or three. Glue to cover the inner basket rim and to hide the wires.

4. Use the ribbon to make a puffy bow with eight 6" (15.2cm) loops, a 14" (35.6cm) and an 18" (45.7cm) tail. Wire the bow to the bottom of the handle front as shown above.

BURGUNDY ROSE BOUQUET

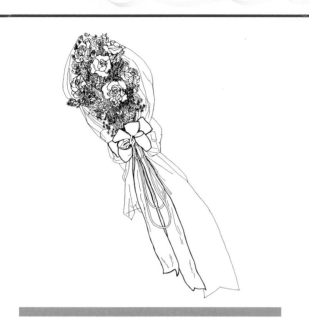

BURGUNDY ROSE BOUQUET

Bouquet Style:
presentation with complementary color harmony

six stems of burgundy satin roses,
each with a 5" (12.7cm) wide blossom and many leaves

5 ounces (141.8g) of preserved green ming fern

three stems of white silk chickweed,
each with four 8" (20.3cm) sprigs of
1½" (3.8cm) wide blossoms

three stems of silk blackberries,
each with two sprigs of five ⅝" (1.6cm) wide
burgundy, red and green berries

two 45" (114.3cm) squares of ivory tulle

3¾ yards (342.6cm) of 6" (15.2cm) wide ivory tulle

3¼ yards (297cm) of 2¾" (7cm) wide burgundy
wire-edged ribbon

3¼ yards (297cm) of ¼" (.6cm)
wide gold lamé cord

½ ounce (14.2g) of natural dried baby's breath

30-gauge wire (for tying bouquet)

22-gauge wire (for bows)

hot glue gun and sticks

gold spray glitter

1. Cut the roses to 23" (58.4cm), 24" (61cm), 25" (63.5cm), 26" (66cm), 28" (71.1cm) and 29" (73.7cm) lengths. Position them on a table at varying lengths; loosely bind with wire. Cut a 30" (76.2cm) ming stem and place it behind the longest rose. Cut more ming stems and insert near roses of the same length. Again, loosely bind the bouquet.

2. Insert chickweed stems so there are chickweed blossoms near each rose. Insert a berry stem near the longest rose (wire to the rose stem if necessary). Insert one berry stem, angled outward, on each side of the bouquet.

3. When all the stems are in place and the bouquet is as full as desired, bind the stems tightly with wire to secure.

4. Place the tulle squares together and cut off a corner, rounding it smoothly. Place the bouquet diagonally on the tulle, with the tallest rose at the rounded corner; bring the sides in to the stems and wrap with wire to secure.

5. Use the 6" (15.2cm) wide tulle to make a puffy bow with six 6" (15.2cm) loops, a 20" (50.8cm) tail and a 34" (86.4cm) tail. Glue to the bouquet stems over the wire. Use the burgundy ribbon to make a puffy bow with six 5" (12.7cm) loops and 24" (61cm) tails; glue it over the tulle bow. Use the cord to make a loopy bow with a center loop, six 4" (10.2cm), a 12" (30.5cm) and a 15" (38.1cm) loop; glue it over the burgundy bow.

6. Cut 6"-12" (15.2cm-30.5cm) baby's breath sprigs; glue them, evenly spaced, among the flowers and fern to add a light, airy look. Spray the entire bouquet with glitter.

This presentation or arm bouquet features materials of complementary colors—red and green are directly opposite each other on the color wheel.

Designer Tip:
Using silk flowers means you can use flowers that are out of season and construct the projects well ahead of time.

PINK MODIFIED WATERFALL

PINK MODIFIED WATERFALL

Bouquet Style:
waterfall with monochromatic color harmony

eleven stems of light pink silk freesia,
each with three 3"-4" (7.6cm-10.2cm) clusters
of blossoms and a bud

foam bouquet holder for silk flowers

two green silk needlepoint ivy,
each with thirteen 4"-18" (10.2cm-45.7cm) branches
of 1" (2.5cm) wide leaves

eleven stems of pink silk roses, each with a 3" (7.6cm)
wide blossom and a bud

5⅓ yards (487.7cm) of 1½" (3.8cm) wide
pink printed chiffon ribbon

12 yards (11m) of 6mm white oval pearl beads

10" (25.4cm) white lace bouquet collar

22-gauge wire (for bows)

18-gauge wire (for stems)

green floral tape

3" (7.6cm) wired wood picks

hot glue gun and sticks

FloraLock spray stem adhesive

1. Cut a 25" (63.5cm) freesia stem; insert it into the center bottom of the holder to hang downward. Cut a 27" (68.6cm) ivy stem and insert it behind the freesia. Cut a 23" (58.4cm) rosebud and insert it in front of the freesia.

2. Cut an 86" (218.4cm) length of ribbon. Form it into an 18" (45.7cm) and a 22" (55.9cm) loop, secure it to a wood pick and insert it into the foam to drape over the flowers. Cut a 110" (279.4cm) length of pearls. Form it into a 13" (33cm), an 18" (45.7cm) and a 21" (53.3cm) loop; attach to a wood pick and insert it over the ribbon loops. Cut a 62" (157.5cm) pearl length and form it into a 17" (43.2cm), a 22" (55.9cm) and a 23" (58.4cm) loop, secure it to a wood pick and insert it to extend over the first pearl loops.

3. Continue to cut and insert flower and ivy stems; gradually make the stems shorter, fill in on each side of the longest stems and work up the bouquet. The shortest stems should be 8"-9" (20.3cm-22.9cm) long. Cut two 48" (121.9cm) pearl lengths. Form each into a 12" (30.5cm), a 17" (43.2cm) and a 19" (48.3cm) loop and attach to a wood pick. Carefully insert the loops to extend among the flowers on each side of the waterfall.

4. Use the ribbon to make a puffy bow with a center loop, eight 4" (10.2cm) loops and 11" (27.9cm) tails. Attach to a wood pick and insert it into the foam center. Cut four 48" (121.9cm) pearl lengths; form each into four 5"-6" (12.7cm-15.2cm) loops and attach to a wood pick. Insert one just above the bow; set the others aside for step 6.

5. Cut a 10" (25.4cm) ivy sprig; insert it into the center top of the holder to extend up and back over the handle. Cut two 9" (22.9cm) freesia stems and insert one on each side of the ivy. Cut 7"-8" (17.8cm-20.3cm) sprigs of ivy, freesia and roses. Insert, evenly spaced, around the edges to angle slightly back and over the remaining foam.

6. Insert a pearl loop pick at the center top to extend back among the upper flowers. Insert another on each side of the bouquet. Carefully spray the foam with adhesive.

This bouquet is very full, with all the pieces layered in, creating a compact, waterfall look. The colors are monochromatic, featuring shades of pink. The stems are inserted into a bouquet holder that has been turned upside down; this provides more stability in the bride's hands for this heavy bouquet.

PURPLE MOUND BOUQUET

Bouquet Style:
round with complementary color harmony

foam bouquet holder for silk flowers

10" (25.4cm) white lace bouquet collar

2 yards (182.9cm) of ⅝" (1.6cm) wide
white acetate ribbon

three stems of pale yellow silk roses,
each with a 2" (5.1cm) wide blossom

4 yards (365.8cm) of 1½" (3.8cm) wide
purple/green shimmering wire-edged ribbon

4½ yards (411.5cm) of ⅜" (1cm) wide
gold mesh wired ribbon

twelve stems of purple silk wild violets, each with a
7" (17.8cm) section of ⅜"–¾" (1cm–1.9cm) wide blossoms

three stems of dusty purple silk daisies,
each with seven 1" (2.5cm) wide blossoms

three stems of white silk Scottish heather,
each with four branches
of three 5"–9" (12.7cm–22.9cm) feathery sprigs

1 ounce (28.4g) preserved isolepsis

white floral tape

hot glue gun and sticks

22-gauge wire (for bows)

2½" (6.4cm) wired wood picks

FloraLock spray stem adhesive

1. Insert the bouquet holder into the collar; wrap the prongs with floral tape to secure. Wrap the handle with white ribbon, beginning at the bottom and gluing the ends to secure.

2. Cut the roses to 4" (10.2cm) lengths. Insert them into the foam in a triangle, each angled toward the outer foam edge. Cut the leaves from the main stems; insert the leaves around the edge as a background for the flowers.

3. Use the purple/green ribbon to make a puffy bow with eight 3" (7.6cm) loops, a 15" (38.1cm) loop and a 17" (43.2cm) tail. Attach to a wood pick, and then insert it into the lower center front of the foam. Use the gold ribbon to make a loopy bow with eight 3½" (8.9cm) loops, a 12" (30.5cm) loop, a 15" (38.1cm) loop and a 10" (25.4cm) tail. Glue it to the purple bow center.

4. Cut each violet stem into two 4" (10.2cm) sprigs. Insert, evenly spaced, around the roses. Cut all the daisies off the main stems and to 4" (10.2cm). Insert in the same fashion as the violets.

5. Hold the gold ribbon over the purple ribbon and handle as one to make a collar bow with two 3" (7.6cm) loops; attach to a wood pick. Repeat to make two more collar bows. Insert one into the foam center, one at the upper left and one at the upper right.

6. Cut each heather stem into four sprigs. Insert, evenly spaced, among all the flowers. Cut the top 5"–6½" (12.7cm–16.5cm) from an isolepsis sprig and wire to a wood pick. Insert into the bouquet among the flowers. Repeat, inserting them, evenly spaced, until the bouquet is very full. Carefully apply stem adhesive to the foam to ensure the stems will not loosen as the bouquet is carried.

The complementary colors purple and yellow are used to construct this round bouquet, also known as a colonial bouquet.

P U R P L E H A N D - T I E D B O U Q U E T

Bouquet Style:
hand - tied with analogous color harmony

two stems of dark purple silk iris,
each with a 5" (12.7cm) tall blossom and a bud

four stems of blue silk daisies,
each with a 9" (22.9cm) section
of ½" (1.3cm) wide blossoms

four stems of lavender silk sweet peas,
each with eight 1½" (3.8cm) tall blossoms

three stems of white satin stephanotis, each with an 11"
(27.9cm) section of twelve 2" (5.1cm) tall blossoms

2 ounces (56.7g) purple dried artemisia

1⅔ yards (152.4cm) of 2¼" (5.7cm) wide
white/blue/lavender wire-edged printed ribbon

2¼ yards (205.7cm) of ⅞" (2.2cm) wide
lavender satin ribbon

1⅔ yards (152.4cm) of 1" (2.5cm) wide
white iridescent flat lace

30 - gauge wire (for tying bouquet)

22- gauge wire (for bow)

hot glue gun and sticks

1. Cut the two iris buds off the main stems, leaving them 12" (30.5cm) long. Cut one open iris to 18" (45.7cm) and one to 15" (38.1cm). Hold them together and add a sweet pea stem to extend 2" (5.1cm) above the tallest iris. Wrap the stems with 30-gauge wire, but do not cut the excess wire.

2. Add two daisy stems, one on each side of the bouquet. Place the three stephanotis stems, evenly spaced, around the bouquet. Place artemisia sprigs around the bouquet; wrap again with wire.

3. Continue adding the remaining flowers and as much artemisia as desired. Wrap the stems securely with wire several times. Arrange the silk flowers by bending the stems as needed to space them evenly throughout the bouquet. Cut 8"-10" (20.3cm-25.4cm) artemisia sprigs and glue them among the flowers in the bouquet center.

4. Trim the stems as needed to make a comfortable handle about 8" (20.3cm) below the lowest flowers. Cut an 18" (45.7cm) lavender ribbon length and glue the center 4" (10.2cm) below the wired area. Wrap the ribbon ends in opposite directions up the stems, crossing them and completely covering the stems and wire; tie the ends to secure.

5. Hold the lace and lavender ribbon together over the white ribbon. Make a collar bow with two 4" (10.2cm) loops and 14"-20" (35.6cm-50.8cm) tails; secure with wire. Cut a 2" (5.1cm) white ribbon length and wrap the bow center, gluing the ends at the back. Glue the bow over the ribbon knot.

Also known as a clutch bouquet, this is a casual hand-tied design using flowers of analogous colors. Blue, blue-violet and violet, used here, are colors that are adjacent on the color wheel.

Designer Tip:
Silk hand-tied bouquets can be enlarged after the bouquet has been tied. Cut flower sprigs to the desired lengths and glue them among the flowers as needed to fill out the design.

CORAL CRESCENT BOUQUET

Bouquet Style:
crescent with monochromatic color harmony

foam bouquet holder for silk flowers

8" (20.3cm) white tulle bouquet collar

2 yards (182.9cm) of ⁵⁄₈" (1.6cm) wide
white acetate ribbon

four stems of coral silk dogwood, each with three
4" (10.2cm) wide blossoms and three buds

four stems of peach silk rosebuds, each with three
sprigs of three 1" (2.5cm) wide blossoms

3³⁄₄ yards (342.9cm) of 1¹⁄₂" (3.8cm) wide
peach moiré ribbon

3³⁄₄ yards (342.9cm) of cream satin cord

1¹⁄₂ ounces (42.5g) preserved tree fern

twelve white pearl sprays, each with two strands
of round and teardrop pearls

green and white floral tape

tacky craft glue

18-gauge wire (for stems)

22-gauge wire (for bows)

3" (7.6cm) wired wood pick

FloraLock floral adhesive

1. Insert the bouquet holder into the collar; wrap the prongs with floral tape to secure. Wrap the handle with white ribbon, beginning at the bottom and gluing the ends to secure. Cut an 18" (45.7cm) dogwood stem, curve it and insert it into the lower right of the foam. Cut a 10" (25.4cm) stem, curve it and insert it into the upper left. Be sure the two stems make the same curving line, forming a crescent.

2. Cut another 10" (25.4cm) stem and insert it to follow the established line, covering the empty area of the lower stem. Cut the remaining stem to 6" (15.2cm) and insert it straight up into the center. Bend the stem of one blossom downward and another upward.

3. Cut a rosebud stem to 14" (35.6cm); insert it near the 18" (45.7cm) dogwood stem. Cut a 10" (25.4cm) rosebud sprig and insert it near the 10" (25.4cm) upper dogwood stem. Cut the remaining rosebud stems into sprigs and insert, evenly spaced, among the dogwood, following the crescent line.

4. Use the peach ribbon to make a puffy bow with eight 5" (12.7cm) loops, a 20" (50.8cm) tail and a 24" (61cm) tail. Attach to a wood pick and insert into the center bottom of the foam. Use the cord to make a loopy bow with four 4"-6" (10.2cm-15.2cm), a 12" (30.5cm) and a 17" (43.2cm) loop and a 24" (61cm) tail. Glue this bow to the center of the peach bow.

5. Cut the tree fern into 7"-20" (17.8cm-50.8cm) sprigs; insert them, evenly spaced, among the flowers, filling empty spaces and providing a backdrop for the coral and peach tones. Floral tape each pearl spray to wire. Cut them into 4"-7" (10.2cm-17.8cm) lengths and insert them, evenly spaced, among the flowers. Spray the foam with adhesive to secure the stems.

A monochromatic color scheme, shades of peach and coral, was used to make this crescent bouquet. Because of its shape, this style allows more of the bride's gown to be seen.

BRIDE'S CASCADE BOUQUET

BRIDE'S CASCADE BOUQUET

foam bouquet holder

8" (20.3cm) cream crocheted bouquet collar

9" (22.9cm) pencil-edge white tulle bouquet collar

2 yards (182.9cm) of ⅝" (1.6cm) wide
white acetate ribbon

one white silk peony bush with five 4" (10.2cm) wide
blossoms, three buds and numerous leaves

4⅓ yards (396.2cm) of 1½" (3.8cm) wide
cream/gold dotted ribbon

two packages of gold Zingers bullion

five stems of mauve silk chickweed,
each with four sprigs
of three 1" (2.5cm) wide blossoms

three stems of white silk Scottish heather,
each with four branches of three 5"-9"
(12.7cm-22.9cm) sprigs with pelletlike blossoms

three brass charms: one 2" (5.1cm) wide
embossed heart, one 1¾" (4.5cm) wide embossed
heart, one 1¾" (4.5cm) wide open heart

cotton swab, black acrylic paint, paper towels,
gloss acrylic spray sealer (to antique charms)

green and white floral tape

hot glue gun and sticks

3" (7.6cm) wired wood picks

one 6" (15.2cm) wood pick

18-gauge wire

22-gauge wire

1. Insert the bouquet holder into the crocheted collar, and then into the tulle collar; wrap the prongs with floral tape to secure. Wrap the handle with white ribbon, beginning at the bottom and gluing the ends to secure.

2. Cut a peony bud to 18" (45.7cm); insert it into the bottom of the foam to extend downward. Cut a 12" (30.5cm) and an 8" (20.3cm) blossom. Insert them in front of the bud, also to extend downward. Cut three 7" (17.8cm) long blossoms and insert them around the foam center in a triangle. Insert a 7" (17.8cm) bud into the foam center and an 8" (20.3cm) bud to extend down and to the left. Insert sprigs of leaves around the outer edge of the foam behind the flowers.

3. Use the cream/gold dotted ribbon to make a puffy bow with six 4" (10.2cm) loops, a 15" (38.1cm) loop, a 17" (43.2cm) tail and a 25" (63.5cm) tail. Attach to a wood pick and insert it into the foam bottom just above the 8" (20.3cm) peony; knot the tails. Stretch one package of bullion to 3 yards (274.3cm); use to make five 14"-20" (35.6cm-50.8cm) long loops. Secure the loops with wire, and then glue them to the bow center.

4. Cut a 17" (43.2cm), a 14" (35.6cm), an 11" (27.9cm) and two 9" (22.9cm) chickweed sprigs; insert them into the bottom of the foam among the longest peonies. Cut the remaining chickweed into 8" (20.3cm) sprigs; insert them, evenly spaced, among the upper flowers.

5. Cut two 9" (22.9cm) heather branches and set aside. Cut the rest of this stem to 20" (50.8cm) and insert it into the bottom of the foam. Cut an 11" (27.9cm) branch and insert it in front of the 20" (50.8cm) stem. Cut the remaining stems into 9" (22.9cm) sprigs; insert them, evenly spaced, among the flowers.

6. Cut three 18" (45.7cm) lengths of cream/gold dotted ribbon. Form each into a collar bow with two 4" (10.2cm) loops and no tails; attach each to a wood pick. Insert one at the upper left and one at the upper right of the foam; insert the third at the foam center. Stretch out the other length of bullion to 4 yards (365.8cm). Make it into ten 8"-15" (20.3cm-38.1cm) loops and attach it to a wood pick; insert it into the bouquet center.

7. Antique and seal the charms. Glue the large heart to the 6" (15.2cm) wood pick and insert it into the foam center. Glue the open heart to a chickweed stem 2" (5.1cm) above the lowest bud; glue the last heart to another stem halfway between the upper and lower hearts.

MAID'S MOUND BOUQUET

MAID'S MOUND BOUQUET

foam bouquet holder

7" (17.8cm) cream crocheted bouquet collar

8" (20.3cm) pencil-edge white tulle bouquet collar

2 yards (182.9cm) of 5/8" (1.6cm) wide
white acetate ribbon

one mauve/green silk begonia bush with at least three
3" (7.6cm) wide and five 2" (5.1cm) wide blossoms,
plus numerous leaves

one stem of mauve silk chickweed with four sprigs
of three 1" (2.5cm) wide blossoms

one stem of white silk chickweed with four sprigs
of three 1" (2.5cm) wide blossoms

two stems of white silk daisies, each with three
10" (25.4cm) sprigs of thirty 1/2" (1.3cm) wide blossoms

3 1/2 yards (320cm) of 2" (5.1cm) wide
mauve/green wire-edged ribbon

3 1/2 yards (320cm) of 3/8" (1cm) wide
metallic gold mesh wired ribbon

1 ounce (28.4g) natural dried baby's breath

one 3" (7.6cm) long brass bird charm

cotton swab, black acrylic paint, paper towels,
gloss acrylic spray sealer (to antique charm)

green and white floral tape

hot glue gun and sticks

3" (7.6cm) wired wood picks

one 6" (15.2cm) wood pick

18-gauge wire (for stems)

22-gauge wire (for bows)

1. Insert the bouquet holder into the crocheted collar, and then into the tulle collar; wrap the prongs with floral tape to secure. Wrap the handle with white ribbon, beginning at the bottom and gluing the ends to secure.

2. Cut three 3" (7.6cm) wide begonia blossoms to 4" (10.2cm) long. Insert them in the foam center, angled outward in a triangle. Cut five 2" (5.1cm) wide blossoms to 4½" (11.4cm) long and insert, evenly spaced, around the outside of the foam, parallel with the collars.

3. Cut 2- or 3-leaf begonia sprigs to 3" (7.6cm) long. Insert them between the blossoms around the edge to provide a background to the design. Insert more leaf sprigs among the center flowers.

4. Cut each chickweed stem into four 7" (17.8cm) sprigs; insert them, evenly spaced, among the begonias. Cut each daisy stem into nine 6"-7" (15.2cm-17.8cm) sprigs. Insert them, evenly spaced, among all the flowers.

5. Cut four 14" (35.6cm) lengths of each colored ribbon. Hold a gold length over a mauve one and make a collar bow with two 3" (7.6cm) loops and no tails. Attach to a 3" (7.6cm) wood pick. Repeat with the remaining 14" (35.6cm) lengths. Insert three bows into the foam, evenly spaced around the outside, with one located at the center bottom. Insert the last bow into the foam center.

6. Cut four 10"-16" (25.4cm-40.6cm) mauve/green ribbon streamers, hold them together and attach one end to a 3" (7.6cm) pick. Insert into the bottom of the foam to extend from below the bow. Cut three 15"-22" (38.1cm-55.9cm) gold streamers and attach to a 3" (7.6cm) pick; insert in front of the mauve streamers.

7. Cut the baby's breath into 6"-8" (15.2cm-20.3cm) sprigs; insert them, evenly spaced, among all the flowers. Antique and seal the bird charm. Glue the 6" (15.2cm) wood pick to the back and insert into the bouquet center.

FLOWER GIRL'S BASKET & HAIR CLIP

B A S K E T

9" (22.9cm) pencil-edge white tulle bouquet collar

9" x 4" (22.9cm x 10.2cm) round basket with a 7" (17.8cm) tall handle

12" (30.5cm) round cream crocheted doily

3½ yards (320cm) of ⅝" (1.6cm) wide
white/gold embroidered ribbon

two 2" (5.1cm) wide mauve begonia blossoms,
each with a 3" (7.6cm) long leaf

eight 1" (2.5cm) wide mauve chickweed blossoms,
each on a 1½" (3.8cm) stem

six 3"-5½" (7.6cm-14cm) sprigs of white Scottish heather

one package of gold Zingers bullion

two 1" (2.5cm) wide brass heart charms

cotton swab, black acrylic paint, paper towels,
gloss acrylic spray sealer (to antique charms)

flower petals, burgundy potpourri and gold fibers to fill the basket

two 8" (20.3cm) lengths of 22-gauge wire (bows)

hot glue gun and sticks

H A I R   C L I P

one 4" (10.2cm) round white Battenberg lace doily

one 6" (15.2cm) round cream crocheted doily

9" (22.9cm) of 1" (2.5cm) wide mauve/green wire-edged ribbon

one stem of mauve silk chickweed with six 1½" (3.8cm) wide blossoms

three 2" (5.1cm) long sprigs of white silk daisies,
each with three ½" (1.3cm) wide blossoms

three 2" (5.1cm) long sprigs of white silk Scottish heather

5" (12.7cm) of gold Zingers bullion

2½" (6.4cm) long spring clip barrette

22-gauge wire

hot glue gun and sticks

Basket:

1. Remove the tulle portion from the bouquet collar and discard the plastic. Glue the gathered tulle around the inside of the basket to extend outward over the rim.

2. Cut a 5" (12.7cm) circle from the doily center and discard. Glue the doily over the tulle, gathering as necessary to fit. Glue the tulle and doily flat over the basket edge. Glue ribbon over the inside doily edges.

3. On one side of the basket, glue a begonia leaf to extend out from the inside edge over the rim. Glue a begonia blossom on the leaf, with four chickweed blossoms around it. Glue a 5½" (14cm) heather sprig to extend over the basket edge and two 3" (7.6cm) sprigs around the begonia.

4. Cut a 1" (2.5cm) bullion length; stretch to 18" (45.7cm) and form into three 1¾"-2¾" (4.5cm-7cm) loops. Twist the ends to secure, and then glue to extend from under the begonia over the heather sprig.

5. Antique and seal the heart charms. Glue an antiqued charm to extend over the bullion. Use the ribbon to make a puffy bow with a center loop, ten 2" (5.1cm) loops and 5" (12.7cm) tails. Glue at the handle base nearest the flowers, but angled away from them. Cut a 2" (5.1cm) bullion length and form into six 2"-3" (5.1cm-7.6cm) loops; twist the ends to secure, and then glue into the bow center, angled upward.

6. Repeat steps 3 through 5 on the opposite side of the basket using the remaining materials. Fill the basket with petals, potpourri and gold fibers.

Hair Clip:

1. Center the small doily over the large one; wrap wire around the center to make a bow. Use the ribbon to make a collar bow with two 2" (5.1cm) loops and no tails; glue this bow over the center of the doily bow.

2. Glue five chickweed blossoms plus the daisy and heather sprigs over the ribbon bow, extending outward from the center.

3. Stretch the bullion to 36" (91.4cm) long. Use to make a loopy bow with 1½"-2" (3.8cm-5.1cm) loops and no tails; twist the center to secure. Glue to the ribbon bow center, and then glue the remaining chickweed blossom over it. Glue the barrette to the back.

MAID'S ORCHID BOUQUET

MAID'S ORCHID BOUQUET

three stems of Phalaenopsis orchids

bouquet holder for fresh flowers

five stems of mauve heather

eight stems of variegated ivy

3 yards (274.3cm) of 3/8" (1cm) wide
metallic gold wired mesh ribbon

3 yards (274.3cm) of cream satin cord

five stems of ming fern

4" (10.2cm) long wired wood picks

1. Insert an 18" (45.7cm) orchid stem into the lower left of the holder to curve down. Insert a 12" (30.5cm) stem into the upper right to extend up. Insert three 4" (10.2cm) sprigs into the foam center.

2. Cut 12"-18" (30.5cm-45.7cm) ivy sprigs. Insert the sprigs to follow the curving line established with the orchids. Fill in between the upper and lower longest ivy sprigs with shorter ivy stems.

3. Hold the ribbon and cord together. Make four 6" (15.2cm) loops of each; wire to a wood pick. Repeat. Insert a loop set into the center to extend forward, and one to the lower left of it.

4. Cut 4"-6" (10.2cm-15.2cm) fern sprigs and 6"-7" (15.2cm-17.8cm) heather sprigs; insert them around the center to cover any exposed foam. Cut four 12"-16" (30.5cm-40.6cm) heather stems and insert them at the lower left around the orchids. Cut four 8"-10" (20.3cm-25.4cm) heather stems and insert them into the upper right to extend among the upper orchids.

5. Fill any empty areas with 5" (12.7cm) ivy sprigs.

ROSE & ALSTROEMERIA BOUQUET

1. Hold the alstroemeria stems together under the blossoms. Hold the roses in a cluster beside them.

2. Place the bear grass beside the roses; loop the ends down to the stems and hold. Place the beaded leaves beside the roses, and the galax leaves under the alstroemeria.

3. Tie the stems under the heads with a 2-yard (182.9cm) length of white ribbon. Wrap a 6" (15.2cm) white ribbon length over the ends of the stems. Glue one end of a 3-yard (274.3cm) length to the 6" (15.2cm) piece at the bottom of the stems. Wrap spiral fashion around the stems, completely covering them; glue at the top.

4. Use the pink/white ribbon to make a puffy bow with four 10"-18" (25.4cm-45.7cm) loops, a 16" (40.6cm) tail and a 32" (81.3cm) tail. Assemble with a 46" (116.8cm) length, and then tie to the bouquet under the flower heads. Tie a 2-yard (182.9cm) tulle length just below the ribbons.

Designer Tips

1. Remove thorns before using roses in a handheld bouquet.

2. To work with open roses, allow them to open to the desired stage. Mix one part white glue and two parts water in a bowl. Dip the head of the rose into the glue mixture, shake to remove excess glue, and place in a vase of water to dry. This will keep the rose from opening more, and keep the outer petals from falling. Do not use this mixture on dark roses, as it will discolor them.

ROSE & ALSTROEMERIA BOUQUET

five stems of alstroemeria

ten stems of hot pink roses

six strands of bear grass

nine 4" (10.2cm) long pearl/beaded leaves

three 3½" (8.9cm) wide green satin galax leaves

7½ yards (685.8cm) of 1½" (3.8cm) wide white wire-edged ribbon

4½ yards (411.5cm) of 1" (2.5cm) wide pink/white wire-edged ribbon

2 yards (182.9cm) of 8" (20.3cm) wide white tulle

low-temperature glue gun and sticks

GARDEN RITES BRIDE'S BOUQUET

GARDEN RITES BRIDE'S BOUQUET

five stems of white silk roses, each with a 4" (10.2cm) wide rose and three leaves

one 11" (27.9cm) white tulle bouquet collar with three pencil-edge layers

one bouquet holder with foam for silks

one stem of green silk ivy with one 30" (76.2cm) and two 18" (45.7cm) branches of many 1½"–3" (3.8cm–7.6cm) wide leaves

one stem of pink silk roses and berries with three 1½" (3.8cm) wide roses, four berries and latex leaves

2½ yards (228.6cm) of 1¼" (3.2cm) wide white lace ribbon

2½ yards (228.6cm) of ½" (1.3cm) wide gold wired mesh braid

two stems of creamy-white/pink silk oncidium orchids, each with a 13" (33cm) and two 9" (22.9cm) sprigs of many ¾"–1½" (1.9cm–3.8cm) wide blossoms

2 ounces (56.7g) 6"–15" (15.2cm–38.1cm) long natural birch twigs

1/2 ounce (14.2g) green sheet moss

three white pearl loop sprays, each with three 6" (15.2cm) loops

two 2" (5.1cm) long wired wood picks

22-gauge wire

mauve acrylic paint and no. 8 angled brush

low-temperature glue gun and sticks

1. Immerse two roses in water; shake. Dip the brush tip in paint and stroke the inside base of each petal. Let dry. Glue the collar on the holder. Cut each 18" (45.7cm) ivy branch into a 10" (25.4cm) and an 8" (20.3cm) sprig, then cut one 10" (25.4cm) sprig in half. Save a 3" (7.6cm) three-leaf sprig from the 30" (76.2cm) branch for step 4. Cut two 3" (7.6cm) and three 6" (15.2cm) sprigs from the remainder. Glue into the foam arranged as shown.

2. Cut a white rose to 6" (15.2cm) and a painted rose to 5" (12.7cm). Glue into the foam bottom as shown. Cut the other roses to 4" (10.2cm); glue into the foam center, angled as shown. Cut a 10" (25.4cm) one-rose, two-berry section and a 7" (17.8cm) one-rose section from the rose and berry stem. Insert into the foam center as shown. Cut a 12" (30.5cm) one-rose, two-berry section; glue it extending downward.

3. Cut 36" (91.4cm) of lace and 45" (114.3cm) of braid. Wire their centers to one wood pick; glue under the 10" (25.4cm) ivy sprig. Cut 45" 114.3cm) of lace; make a collar bow with 3" (7.6cm) loops, a 12" (30.5cm) tail and a 16" (40.6cm) tail. With 42" (106.7cm) of braid, make a collar bow with 2½" (6.4cm) loops and 12" (30.5cm) knotted tails. Wire the braid bow over the lace bow on a wood pick; glue to the foam center. Trim one orchid stem to 17" (43.2cm); trim the other to 15" (38.1cm). Insert each into the foam center, with the longest sprig angled down and a short one to each side.

4. Glue the ivy sprig (from step 1) to the bow center. Cut remaining rose leaves with 1" (2.5cm) stems; glue into empty spaces. Glue the twigs near flowers of similar lengths. Glue moss over any exposed foam. Insert the pearl loops around the bow.

G A R D E N   R I T E S
M A I D ' S   B O U Q U E T

one 10" (25.4cm) round white Battenberg lace doily
with scalloped edges

one bouquet holder with foam for silks

four stems of pink silk roses, each with
one 4" (10.2cm) wide rose and leaves

one stem of white silk Scottish heather with
four 7" (17.8cm) three-sprig feathery branches
of pellet-like blossoms

1½ yards (137.2cm) of 1¼" (3.2cm) wide
pink/gold floral print ribbon

1¾ yards (160cm) of 6mm white oval fused beads

½ yard (45.7cm) of 1⅜" (3.5cm) wide
white wired mesh ribbon

one stem of burgundy silk gardenias with
nine 2" (5.1cm) sprigs of one to two 1½" (3.8cm) wide
blossoms and buds

eleven 10" (25.4cm) long natural birch twigs

½ ounce (14.2g) preserved green plumosus fern

22-gauge wire

four 2" (5.1cm) wired wood picks

low-temperature glue gun and sticks

1. Cut and discard the 1¼" center circle from the doily. Slide the doily over the holder handle and glue to the back of the holder. Cut the roses with 2" (5.1cm) stems. Glue into the foam as shown. Cut the heather into four 7" (17.8cm) branches; bend each sprig into a loop. Glue three sprigs around the sides and one near the center rose.

2. Cut three 8" (20.3cm) and two 15" (38.1cm) lengths of floral ribbon. Fold each 8" (20.3cm) length in half, wire the ends and attach to a pick; insert them around the center rose. Loop the beads into a 7" (17.8cm) and a 9" (22.9cm) loop with a 12" (30.5cm) tail and a 14" (35.6cm) tail; wire to secure. Wire the 15" (38.1cm) floral ribbon lengths, the mesh ribbon and the bead loops to a wood pick and glue to extend down from under the lowest rose. Knot the mesh ribbon end.

3. Insert nine 2" (5.1cm) gardenia sprigs evenly among the roses. Insert six rose leaves around the outside foam edge against the doily, and one on each side of the center rose. Glue other leaves to fill any holes.

4. Make eleven twig loops by bending each twig and wiring the ends to secure. Glue five twig loops around the center rose, and six around the outside of the bouquet, against the doily. Glue 5" (12.7cm) plumosus sprigs, evenly spaced, among the flowers.

SPIDER PLANT BOUQUET

1. Insert galax leaves around the outside of the bouquet holder to conceal the holder.

2. Insert a 20" (50.8cm) spider plant stem into the foam to extend downward. Insert five 8" (20.3cm) sprigs to radiate from the center. Cut and insert mingeri in the same manner as the spider plant.

3. Cut the roses to 4"-6" (10.2cm-15.2cm) long; insert them into the foam, centering as shown. Insert the silk leaves, evenly spaced, among the roses to radiate out from the center. Repeat with the grape leaves and the pearl loops.

4. Use the tulle to make a puffy bow with three 6" (15.2cm) loops, two 8" (20.3cm) tails, a 26" (66cm) tail, a 36" (91.4cm) tail and a 15" (38.1cm) loop. Attach the bow to a wood pick and insert it into the left side of the bouquet.

SPIDER PLANT BOUQUET

one bunch of galax leaves

foam bouquet holder

six stems of spider plant

two bunches of mingeri fern

twelve stems of bridal pink roses

eight 3" (7.6cm) long iridescent white silk fern leaves

six 1" (2.5cm) long pearlized plastic grape leaves

six pearl sprays, each with three 1" (2.5cm) wide loops

4 yards (365.8cm) of 8" (20.3cm) wide white tulle

4" (10.2cm) long wired wood picks

ORCHID AND SMILAX BOUQUET

ORCHID AND SMILAX BOUQUET

one bunch of galax leaves

bouquet holder for fresh flowers

three white cattleya orchids with yellow lips

one 40" (101.6cm) smilax garland

three 3" (7.6cm) long pearl/beaded leaves

7½ yards (685.8cm) of cream satin cord

7½ yards (685.8cm) of ⅜" (1cm) wide
metallic gold wired mesh ribbon

two 12" (30.5cm) iridescent white fabric
leaf/bead stems

one bunch of ming fern

4" (10.2cm) long wired wood picks

22-gauge wire

1. Insert galax leaves around the edge of the foam.

2. Floral tape an orchid to an 18" (45.7cm) wire and insert it into the bottom of the foam. Bend it to extend forward and slightly left. Insert a 6" (15.2cm) orchid to extend forward and down, and another to extend up behind it.

3. Insert the smilax into the upper left of the foam, bring it to the right side and pin it under the orchid, allowing the end to drape down. Wrap this end around the wired orchid stem; let it extend beside the stem.

4. Insert three beaded leaves into the right of the foam to extend horizontally.

5. Hold the cord and ribbon together; make a puffy bow with four 4½"-6" (11.4cm-15.2cm) loops and wire to a wood pick. Insert horizontally into the right side of the bouquet. Make another and insert it into the left side. Make a third with 16"-29" (40.6cm-73.7cm) loops; insert it to hang down just left of the orchid.

6. Shape the leaf/bead stems. Insert one into the upper right and one into the lower left; gently curve the stems into a crescent. Cut the ming into 4"-6" (10.2cm-15.2cm) sprigs and insert them around the orchids to hide the foam.

Designer Tip:
To add a long wire stem to an orchid, place two 22-gauge wires on each side of the orchid stem and floral tape this unit to the end of the wires. Insert the stem into the bottom of the holder and up through the top; bend the end into a hook and gently pull the stem back down just far enough to catch the hook over the upper plastic portion of the foam holder.

CANDLELIGHT BRIDE'S BOUQUET

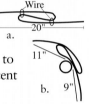

CANDLELIGHT BRIDE'S BOUQUET

two 17" (43.2cm) stems of ivory silk roses, each with
two 2½" (6.4cm) wide roses and one bud

three 10" (25.4cm) long white
beaded sprays, each with twenty
3" (7.6cm) long six-bead sprigs

one 9" (22.9cm) ecru lace bouquet collar

one bouquet holder with foam for silks

one 33" (83.8cm) ivory silk magnolia swag
with three 6"–7" (15.2cm–17.8cm) wide blossoms,
a bud on each end and many green/brown leaves

1⅔ yards (152.4cm) of 2¼" (5.7cm) wide
cocoa/gold organza ribbon

2 yards (182.9cm) of 1¼" (3.2cm) wide beige lace ribbon

1⅔ yards (152.4cm) of ¼" (.6cm) wide ivory cording

one stem of flocked nuts with five 4" (10.2cm) sprigs
of two to three ¾" (1.9cm) wide nuts
and brown silk leaves

three 24" (61cm) long brown pheasant feathers

1½ ounces (42.5g) sage green dried Avena

¼ ounce (7.1g) (seven stems) natural dried Lagurus
(bunny tails)

¾ ounce (21.3g) green sheet moss

copper spray paint

22-gauge wire

low-temperature glue gun and sticks

1. Lightly spray roses and beads with paint;
reserve for step 3. Slip the collar up the
handle of the holder and glue in place. (a)
Bend the swag in a 20" (50.8cm) S curve; wire to
secure; shape into a crescent. (b) Glue the crescent
over the top right curve of the foam cage.

2. Cut and reserve 15" (38.1cm) of organza ribbon; fold each
end of remaining ribbon in a 6" (15.2cm) loop and wire to
secure. Glue one loop to base of the right magnolia bud and
weave the ribbon among the flowers. Glue the other loop to
base of the left magnolia bud. Glue reserved 15" (38.1cm) to
the lower right of the foam. With lace ribbon, make a puffy
bow with two 7" (17.8cm) loops, a 16" (40.6cm) tail and an
18" (45.7cm) tail. Loop the cording into an 8" (20.3cm) and
an 11" (27.9cm) loop with a 16" (40.6cm) knotted tail; wire
to secure. Glue bows below the lower magnolias.

3. Cut a 10" (25.4cm) six-nut sprig and angle downward to
the right; insert a 10" (25.4cm) six-nut sprig angling up and
left from foam. Cut a 6" (15.2cm) rosebud; glue 1" (2.5cm)
below bow center, extending down. Cut the other to 10"
(25.4cm); glue 9" (22.9cm) left of bow center, angling upward
left. Cut two 8" (20.3cm) roses; glue one 2" (5.1cm) right and
up from bow, angling down, and the other 7" (17.8cm) left of
bow center, angling up. Cut two 5" (12.7cm); glue 1" (2.5cm)
and 4" (10.2cm), respectively, left of bow center, extending up.

4. Cut a 10" (25.4cm), a 13" (33cm) and a 14" (35.6cm)
feather tip; cut a 7" (17.8cm) and a 4" (10.2cm) feather base.
Trim cut ends at an angle. Glue tips at the bow center; insert
both bases to extend near upper bud. Cut 7"–14"
(17.8cm–35.6cm) Avena sprigs and 6"–12" (15.2cm–30.5cm)
Lagurus sprigs. Glue sprigs, evenly spaced, among flowers.
Glue moss over any exposed foam. Insert one beaded spray
angling upward left and the others downward right.

TOSSER BOUQUET

TOSSER BOUQUET

8½" (21.6cm) white organza bouquet collar

bouquet holder for silk flowers

two stems of white silk roses,
each with two 2½" (6.4cm) wide roses
and one 1½" (3.8cm) open bud

one 6" (15.2cm) and one 9" (22.9cm) silk ivy sprig,
each with 1⅛"–2" (2.9cm–5.1cm) long leaves

½ ounce (14.2g) green sprengeri

1 ounce (28.4g) white dried baby's breath

three 3" (7.6cm) long white pearl loops

2⅓ yards (213.4cm) of 1½" (3.8cm) wide
white sheer ribbon

2⅔ yards (243.8cm) of 1/16" (.2cm) wide
white satin ribbon

3" (7.6cm) long floral pick with wire

basic supplies (see page 6)

1. Place the collar on the holder. Cut each rose blossom and bud stem to 2" (5.1cm) long, and then glue a 2½" (6.4cm) blossom in the center of the holder. Glue another blossom below it and two above. Glue a bud to each side of the center rose.

2. Cut the ivy into five 3" (7.6cm) sprigs and glue them to extend out between each outer rose. Cut the sprengeri into 2"–3" (5.1cm–7.6cm) sprigs and use them to fill empty space around the ivy and roses.

3. Cut the baby's breath into 2"–3" (5.1cm–7.6cm) sprigs and glue them, evenly spaced, in the bouquet. Glue one pearl loop above the center rose and two below, 3" (7.6cm) apart.

4. Use the sheer ribbon to make a loopy bow with four 4" (10.2cm) loops and 19" (48.3cm) tails. Use the satin ribbon to make a loopy bow with six 4" (10.2cm) loops, an 18" (45.7cm) tail and a 20" (50.8cm) tail. Hold the satin bow over the center of the sheer bow and wire both to the pick. Cut the pick to 2" (5.1cm) and glue it into the lower right of the bouquet.

Keep your bridal bouquet; you can make a silk tosser bouquet for less money than a fresh bouquet, and your guest can keep it as a memento.

Veils & Headpieces

VEIL EDGES & MORE
IVORY LACE CROWN
SATIN FLOWER WREATH
PILLBOX HAT
VICTORIAN PICTURE HAT
LACE & PEARS
BRIDAL HEADBAND
FRENCH WIRE HEADBAND
APPLIQUED HEADBAND
FLOWER GIRL WREATH
GARDEN RITES MAID'S HAT
BRIDAL HEADPIECE
MAID'S HEADPIECE
MAID'S SATIN HAT
BRIDE'S ROSE HEADBAND
LACE HEADPIECE WITH
FINGERTIP VEIL
CANDLELIGHT BRIDE'S
HEADPIECE

VEIL EDGES & MORE

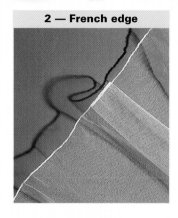
1 — Plain

2 — French edge

EDGING

1. *Plain* — The easiest method. Trim carefully so the edges are smooth.

2. *French edge* — A rolled and stitched edge seen most often in bridal magazines. It can be done well using a serger with a rolled hem plate.

3. *Pearls* — Fused pearls can be hand stitched or zigzagged to the edge.

4. *Ribbon* — Use ¼" (.6cm) wide white, ivory or pastel ribbon and carefully stitch to the edge.

5. *Lace* — Use ⅜"–½" (1cm–1.3cm) wide lace to complement the dress. Stitch to the veil edge.

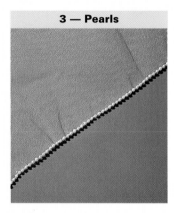
3 — Pearls

4 — Ribbon

POUFS

6. *Bridal* — Use a 12" x 72" (30.5cm x 182.9cm) piece of ivory or white tulle. Fold the tulle in half lengthwise and sew a running stitch joining the open edges. Gather to the width called for and hand stitch to the headpiece.

7. *Communion* — Use a 6" x 72" (15.2cm x 182.9cm) piece of white tulle. Fold the tulle in half lengthwise and sew a running stitch joining the open edges. Gather to 7" (17.8cm) wide, then stitch to the headpiece.

5 — Lace

6 — Bridal pouf

BLUSHER

8. Measure from the crown of the head to the bust line and cut that length from 45" (114.3cm) wide tulle. Round the corners. Sew a running stitch along one edge and gather to 1"–2" (2.5cm–5.1cm). Stitch or glue the hook side of a 1" (2.5cm) length of Velcro to the inside center back of the headpiece. Stitch the loop side to the gathered end of the tulle. Attach the Velcro pieces together.

7 — Communion pouf

8 — Blusher

IVORY LACE CROWN

IVORY LACE CROWN

21" (53.3cm) length of ¼" (.6cm) wide
fabric-covered boning

1 yard (91.4cm) of 6" (15.2cm) wide ivory tulle

½ yard (45.7cm) of 1⅞" (4.8cm) wide
ivory crownlike Venice or Alençon lace

liquid fabric stiffener

⅓ yard (30.5cm) of 72" (182.9cm) wide ivory tulle

1 yard (91.4cm) of 108" (274.3cm) wide ivory tulle

3" (7.6cm) wide clear plastic comb

about seventy-five white 4mm pearls

about fifty-five 5mm–8mm iridescent sequins

needle and ivory thread

no. 8 flat paintbrush

clothes hanger and clothespins

low-temperature glue gun and sticks

1. Measure to fit the bride's head, then cut the boning with 1" (2.5cm) extra. Glue or stitch the ends together, overlapping them 1" (2.5cm). Wrap the boning with the 6" (15.2cm) wide tulle. Glue the lace, with the points up, starting 3"–3½" (7.6cm–8.9cm) from the center back of the boning.

2. Mix five parts stiffener with one part water and use the paintbrush to apply the solution to the lace. Work it in with your fingers. Attach to the hanger with clothespins and let dry with the lace upside down.

3. Use the 72" (182.9cm) wide tulle to make a pouf. Gather to 6" (15.2cm) and stitch at the crown back.

4. With the 108" (274.3cm) tulle make a type 3 veil (see page 8). Gather the veil to 6" (15.2cm) and stitch below the pouf. Sew the comb in the center back of the headpiece. Glue pearls and sequins to the lace. Glue extra pearls and sequins randomly to the veil and pouf.

SATIN FLOWER WREATH

S A T I N   F L O W E R
W R E A T H

24" (61cm) of 18-gauge white cloth-covered wire

3 1/3 (304.8cm) yards of 6" (15.2cm) wide white tulle

two white satin bridal sprays, each with an
18" (45.7cm) section of twelve 2" (5.1cm) wide roses

1 1/4 yards (114.3cm) of 3/8" (1cm) wide
white satin ribbon

1 yard (91.4cm) of 108" (274.3cm) wide white tulle

two white pearl sprays,
each with three 3" (7.6cm) sprigs
of 4mm pearls

two white pearl loop sprays,
each with three 1 1/2" (3.8cm) loops
of 3mm pearls

two 3/4" (1.9cm) long white silk rose buds

3" (7.6cm) wide clear plastic comb

needle and white thread

low-temperature glue gun and sticks

1. Bend the wire to form a circle fitting the bride's head. Twist the ends to secure. Wrap and glue 1 yard (91.4cm) of the 6" (15.2cm) wide tulle around the wire.

2. Lay the bridal sprays side by side and twist the ends together to form one spray. Center it along the wire and use the satin ribbon to wrap the spray to the wire, leaving a 5" (12.7cm) opening at the back. Glue the ribbon ends to secure. With the 108" (274.3cm) tulle, make a type 3 veil (see page 8). Gather the veil to 5" (12.7cm) and stitch to the wire between the bridal spray ends.

3. Use the remaining 6" (15.2cm) wide tulle to make a puffy bow with six 5"–6" (12.7cm–15.2cm) loops and 9" (22.9cm) tails. Glue at the center back of the wire.

4. Glue two 3" (7.6cm) pearl sprays at the bow center, one extending toward each side. Glue a pearl loop spray over each pearl spray. Glue the rosebuds to cover the pearl spray ends. Stitch the comb at the center back.

Note: For a matching flower girl headpiece, see page 52.

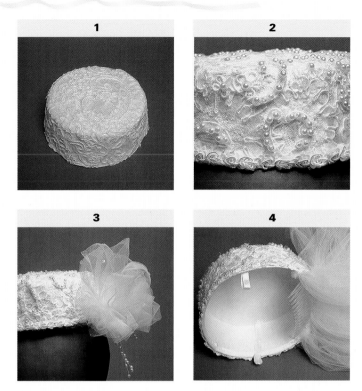

PILLBOX HAT

¹/₈ yard (11.4cm) of 36" (91.4cm) wide white Alençon lace

5⁷/₈" (14.9cm) wide white satin pillbox hat

1³/₄ yards (160cm) of ³/₈" (1cm) wide white sequin and satin braid

about 265 4mm white pearls

about 190 5mm iridescent white sequins

about sixty 2–5mm iridescent white bugle beads

3 yards (274.3cm) of 6" (15.2cm) wide white tulle

two white pearl sprays, each with three 3" (7.6cm) sprigs of 4mm pearls

1 yard (91.4.cm) of 108" (274.3cm) wide white tulle

3" (7.6cm) wide clear plastic comb

¹/₃ yard (30.5cm) of ³/₈" (1cm) wide white satin ribbon

no. 8 flat paintbrush

needle and white thread

clear-drying fabric glue

low-temperature glue gun and sticks

1. Cut the lace into 2"–3" (5.1cm–7.6cm) wide appliqués. Brush fabric glue on the back of each and glue to cover the hat.

2. Glue the braid trim around the hat base. Glue pearls, sequins and bugle beads on the lace to embellish. Follow the design of the lace, if desired.

3. Use the 6" (15.2cm) tulle to make an oblong bow with twelve 2½"–4½" (6.4cm–11.4cm) loops and no tails. Stitch the bow to the hat back. Glue any extra sequins into the loops. Glue the pearl sprays beneath the bow, extending out, with one angled toward each side.

4. Make a type 3 veil (see page 8) with the 108" (274.3cm) tulle. Gather to 5" (12.7cm) and stitch to the inside back of the hat. Stitch the comb over the veil. Cut the ribbon in half, fold each half and glue into loops. Glue to each inner hat side, extending ½" (1.3cm) from the hat bottom.

V I C T O R I A N
P I C T U R E   H A T

1 yard (91.4cm) of 108" (274.3cm) wide white tulle

12" (30.5cm) wide white satin hat with a shirred brim

two white satin bridal sprays,
each with three pearl loop sprays,
a 2½" (6.4cm) wide rose
and 6" (15.2cm) of five 1½" (3.8cm) wide
blossoms and a bud

½ yard (45.7cm) of 1⅝" (4.1cm) wide
white scalloped Alençon lace

6" (15.2cm) of ⅜" (1cm) wide white satin ribbon

needle and white thread

4" (10.2cm) length of white Velcro

low -temperature glue gun and sticks

1. With the 108" (274.3cm) tulle make a type 3 veil (see page 8). Gather the veil to 4" (10.2cm) wide. Stitch the hook side of the Velcro to the gather, and glue the loop side to the brim back just below the crown. Attach the veil.

2. Glue the bridal sprays to the back just above the veil edge, with one extending forward on each crown side.

3. Center the lace around the crown front and glue, hiding the lace ends under the bridal sprays.

4. Cut the ribbon in half. Fold each piece and glue to form a loop. Glue them inside the hat with one on each side, extending ½" (1.3cm) from the hat brim.

LACE AND PEARLS

L A C E   A N D   P E A R L S

two 24" (61cm) lengths of white
cloth-covered 18-gauge wire

2 yards (182.9cm) of 6" (15.2cm) wide white tulle

1½ yards (137.2cm) of 4mm white fused pearls

1½ yards (137.2cm) of 4mm opalescent pearls

twenty-eight 2.5mm silver beads

seven 6mm white pearls

1½ yards (137.2cm) of 72" (182.9cm) wide white tulle

55" (139.7cm) length of 108" (274.3cm) wide white tulle

3" (7.6cm) wide clear plastic comb

1⅔ yards (152.4cm) of 1¾" (4.5cm) wide
white gathered lace

two white pearl loop sprays,
each with three 1½" (3.8cm) loops
of 3mm pearls

four white pearl sprays, each with
three 3" (7.6cm) sprigs of 4mm pearls

needle and white thread

no. 8 flat paintbrush

iridescent glitter

clear-drying fabric glue

low-temperature glue gun and sticks

1. Hold the wire lengths together and bend to form a circle fitting the bride's head. Twist the ends to secure. Bend one side of the circle upward as shown and wrap with the 6" (15.2cm) wide tulle. Holding both fused pearl strands together, wrap the wire and glue, covering the front half as shown. Trim off the extra pearl lengths and save for step 2.

2. Wrap and glue the opalescent strand from step 1 spiral fashion over the first pearl layer. Repeat with the white strand, beginning at the other side and wrapping in the opposite direction. Glue four silver beads around each X formed by the last two strands and one 6mm pearl to the center.

3. Use the 72" (182.9cm) tulle to make a 7" (17.8cm) pouf. With the 108" (274.3cm) tulle make a type 4 veil (see page 8). Gather the veil to 7" (17.8cm) wide. Stitch the pouf and veil at the wire back as shown. Sew the comb at the center back.

4. For rosettes: Cut the lace into three 20" (50.8cm) lengths. Sew a running stitch along the bound edge of each and pull to gather tightly. Stitch the ends of the lace together to form a circle, then stitch the circle hole closed. Brush the petals with fabric glue and lightly sprinkle with glitter. Glue or sew the rosettes, evenly spaced, along the wire where the veil and pouf meet. Glue the pearl loop sprays between the rosettes and a 4mm spray on each side as shown. Cut the remaining 4mm sprays apart and glue two stems into each rosette for stamens.

BRIDAL HEADBAND

BRIDAL HEADBAND

15" x 4" (38.1cm x 10.2cm) piece of cotton batting

2" (5.1cm) wide white or clear plastic headband

17" x 4 1/2" (43.2cm x 11.4cm) piece of white satin

1/2 yard (45.7cm) of 1 1/4" (3.2cm) wide white flat lace

2/3 yard (61cm) of 4 1/2" (11.4cm) wide
white Venice lace floral appliqués

about sixty 4mm white pearls

about eighty 5mm–8mm iridescent sequins

about thirty-five 3mm x 6mm oval white pearls

3/4 yard (68.6cm) of 108" (274.3cm) wide white tulle

needle and white thread

low-temperature glue gun and sticks

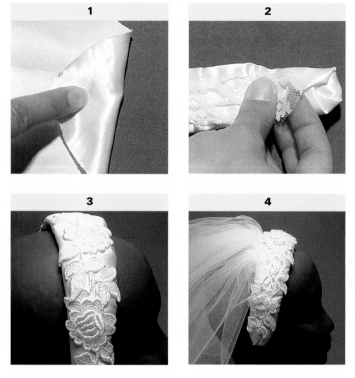

1. Fold the batting in half lengthwise and glue to the headband. Center the satin over the headband. Fold the excess under each short end and glue to secure.

2. Glue one satin long edge along the underside of the headband. Fold the other long edge under, then glue it securely over the first edge at the back. Glue the flat lace over the seam.

3. Cut the appliqués apart. Glue symmetrically over the headband, overlapping the ones near the top if needed. (You may want to pin the appliqués in place before you start gluing to make sure of the fit.)

4. Glue the 4mm pearls in the appliqué flower centers. Glue the sequins and 3mm x 6mm pearls on the leaves and petals. With the 108" (274.3cm) tulle make a type 3 veil (see page 8). Gather to 5" (12.7cm) wide. Stitch the veil to the underside of the headband back.

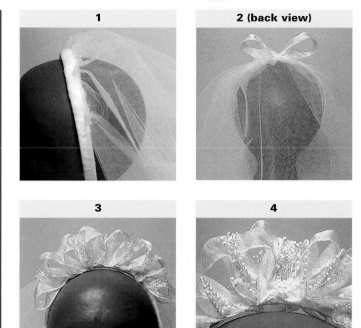

FRENCH WIRE HEADBAND

1/4" (.6cm) wide white or clear plastic headband

1 yard (91.4cm) of 6" (15.2cm) wide white tulle

45" (114.3cm) length of 54" (137.2cm) wide white tulle

1 1/3 yards (121.9cm) of 1 3/8" (3.5cm) wide opalescent white wire-edged ribbon

1/4 ounce (7.1g) of iridescent-glittered white baby's breath

24" (61cm) length of 4mm white fused pearls

seven 6mm white pearls

low-temperature glue gun and sticks

1. Wrap the headband with the 6" (15.2cm) wide tulle; glue the ends at the back to secure. Use the 54" (137.2cm) tulle to make a type 2 veil (see page 8). Gather the veil to 7" (17.8cm) and glue along the back of the headband.

2. Cut the ribbon into eight 6" (15.2cm) lengths. Fold each piece in half and glue the ends, forming a 3" (7.6cm) loop. Glue two loops at the headband center top, one extending to each side.

3. Glue a second loop just below the first on each side. Repeat for four loops on each side. Cut the baby's breath into 2" (5.1cm) sprigs and glue between the loops.

4. Cut eight 3" (7.6cm) pearl lengths and fold each in half to form a loop. Glue the ends. Glue a pearl loop over each ribbon loop. Glue the 6mm pearls in a cluster between the first two loops, covering the ends.

APPLIQUÉD HEADBAND

1" (2.5cm) wide white or clear plastic headband

1 yard (91.4cm) of 6" (15.2cm) wide white tulle

45" (114.3cm) length of 54" (137.2cm) wide white tulle

three 2½"–3½" (6.4cm–8.9cm) wide pearl/iridescent sequined appliqués

⅓ yard (30.5cm) of ⅜" (1cm) wide white sequin and satin braid

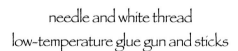

needle and white thread

low-temperature glue gun and sticks

FLOWER GIRL WREATH

Note: This design matches the Satin Flower Wreath on page 46.

18"–20" (45.7cm–50.8cm) length of white cloth-covered 18-gauge wire

3 yards (274.3cm) of 6" (15.2cm) wide white tulle

white satin bridal spray with a 16" (40.6cm) section of nine 2" (5.1cm) wide roses

1 yard (91.4cm) of ⅜" (1cm) wide white satin ribbon

one ¾" (1.9cm) long white silk rosebud

two white pearl sprays, each with three 3" (7.6cm) sprigs of 4mm pearls

needle and white thread

3" (7.6cm) wide clear plastic comb

low-temperature glue gun and sticks

---

1. Wrap the headband with 6" (15.2cm) tulle. With the 54" (137.2cm) tulle make a type 1 veil (see page 8). Gather the veil to 7" (17.8cm) and glue along the center back. Center the largest appliqué at the center front and glue. Glue a remaining appliqué on each side.

2. Cut the braid trim in half. Glue one piece to each side, beginning at the edge of the last appliqué. Fold the end over the edge of the headband to finish and glue.

1. Bend the wire to form a circle fitting the head and wrap with one yard of tulle. Attach the bridal spray to the circle by wrapping ribbon around the stem and wire; glue to secure.

2. Use the remaining tulle to make a puffy bow with six 2½"–4" (6.4cm–10.2cm) loops and 16" (40.6cm) tails. Glue between the bridal spray ends at the back. Glue the rosebud to the bow center. Glue a pearl spray to extend from each side of the rose. Stitch the comb at the center back.

GARDEN RITES MAID'S HAT

G A R D E N   R I T E S
M A I D ' S   H A T

1½ yards (137.2cm) of 1¼" (3.2cm) wide
pink/gold floral print ribbon

one 12" (30.5cm) straw hat

one 10" (25.4cm) round white Battenberg lace doily
with scalloped edges

two stems of pink silk roses, each with
one 4" (10.2cm) wide rose and leaves

burgundy silk gardenias: three 2" (5.1cm) wide
blossoms and two ½" (1.3cm) wide buds,
each on a 1" (2.5cm) stem

three 7" (17.8cm) long feathery sprigs of white silk
Scottish heather with pellet-like blossoms

six 9" (22.9cm) long natural birch twigs

one white pearl loop spray with six
2"–4" (5.1cm–10.2cm) long loops of 3mm beads

¼ ounce (7.1g) green preserved plumosus fern

22-gauge wire

low-temperature glue gun and sticks

1. Glue ¾ yard (68.6cm) of the ribbon around the hat brim with the ends 2½" (6.4cm) right of the hat front center (as worn). Wire the edge of the brim to the crown at the same spot. Cut out and discard the doily's 1½" (3.8cm) center circle. Fold the doily in half with the right sides together; slide it between the brim and the crown, centered at the wire. Glue it in place with the scallops extending 3" (7.6cm) over the crown and 3" (7.6cm) over the outer hat brim.

2. With ¾ yard (68.6cm) of the ribbon, make a puffy bow with four 2½" (6.4cm) loops and no tails. Glue it centered on the doily over the outer hat brim. Cut the rose stems to ½" (1.3cm). Glue one at the bow center and the other above and right of it. Remove the rose leaves from the stems. Glue one rose to each side of the bow center and four behind the brim; glue a small leaf behind the center rose. Reserve 7 to 8 leaves for step 3.

3. Glue one gardenia blossom plus one bud to each side of the center rose, and glue one blossom 1" (2.5cm) above it. Shape each of the heather sprigs into a loop and glue, evenly spaced, around the center rose. Glue the reserved rose leaves evenly among the flowers.

4. Bend one twig in a loop; wire the ends. Repeat for all the twigs. Glue four loops behind the center rose, two extending to each side, and two behind the brim, one extending to each side. Glue the bead spray behind the center rose, with the loops spread around the rose. Glue 2"–4" (5.1cm–10.2cm) plumosus sprigs, evenly spaced, among the flowers.

BRIDAL HEADPIECE

B R I D A L   H E A D P I E C E

3³⁄₄ yards (342.9cm) of 54" (137.2cm) wide
ivory tulle

1 yard (91.4cm) of 4mm white fused pearls

nine pearl loop stems,
each with a 1" (2.5cm) loop of white pearls

3" (7.6cm) clear plastic hair comb

3¹⁄₂ yards (320cm) of 2³⁄₄" (7cm) wide
wire-edged cream lace ribbon

3¹⁄₂ yards (320cm) of 1¹⁄₂" (3.8cm) wide
ivory/gold dotted ribbon

three 3" (7.6cm) wide ivory satin roses

one stem of white silk Scottish heather
with four branches of three 4"-8"
(10.2cm-20.3cm) feathery sprigs

¹⁄₄ ounce (7.1g) natural dried baby's breath

gold spray glitter

rhinestone tiara

gold acrylic paint

soft paintbrush

paper towels

22-gauge white wire

30-gauge silver wire (for step 7)

needle and white thread

hot glue gun and sticks

1. Cut the tulle into an 86" (218.4cm) and a 49"
(124.5cm) length. Fold one end of the 86" (218.4cm)
length down 37" (94cm). Fold down 20" (50.8cm) of the
49" (124.5cm) length; position it over the first piece with
the folded edges even. Measure 8" (20.3cm) from the
folds and pinch across the width of all layers; wire loosely
to make a 4" (10.2cm) wide wrapped area.

2. Thread the needle. Stitch through all the layers across
the wired area to keep it from shifting.

3. Brush the fused pearls and pearl loops with gold paint,
then wipe with paper towels; let dry. Glue fused pearls to
cover the wired area of the tulle. Glue the comb to the
underside of the veil, centered over the pearls. To make
loops for pinning the veil onto the bride's head, insert a
2" (5.1cm) wire length through all layers at each end of
the wired area. Twist the ends to form ½" (1.3cm) wide
loops, cutting off the excess.

4. Use the lace ribbon to make a puffy bow with six 4½"
(11.4cm) loops, a 30" (76.2cm) tail and a 35" (88.9cm)
tail. Glue over the wire on the veil back. Use the dotted
ribbon to make a puffy bow with eight 3¾" (9.5cm)
loops, a 25" (63.5cm) tail and a 27" (68.6cm) tail. Glue
it with the center just below the lace bow's center.

5. Glue a rose angled downward from the gold bow
center; glue one above it angled right. Glue the third
below the center rose angled right, forming a crescent
line. Glue a 3-sprig 7" (17.8cm) heather branch under the
lower rose and another under the upper rose, angled in
the same direction as the roses. Cut the remaining heather
sprigs to 4"-6" (10.2cm-15.2cm) and glue, evenly spaced,
among the roses.

6. Glue three pearl loops at varying lengths under the
lower rose and three under the upper rose. Glue three
more evenly spaced between the roses. Cut the baby's
breath into 4"-8" (10.2cm-20.3cm) sprigs; glue, evenly
spaced, among all the flowers and pearls. Spray the
headpiece with gold glitter.

7. Use the silver wire to attach one end of the remaining
fused pearls to one side of the tiara. Wrap the length
spiral fashion across the horizontal band of the tiara,
wiring the end at the other side and trimming the excess.
Position the tiara on the head; secure the veil at the back
using hairpins through the loops.

MAID'S HEADPIECE

M A I D ' S   H E A D P I E C E

white and silver pearl/bead braided headband

1 yard (91.4cm) of 1/4" (.6cm) wide white satin ribbon

2 yards (182.9cm) of 9" (22.9cm) wide white tulle

1 yard (91.4cm) of 2 3/4" (7cm) wide
cream wire-edged lace ribbon

two 2" (5.1cm) wide mauve silk begonia blossoms
and one 3" (7.6cm) long leaf

one stem of white silk chickweed
with eight 1" (2.5cm) wide blossoms

five 3" (7.6cm) sprigs of white silk daisies,
each with three 1/2" (1.3cm) wide blossoms

one white pearl/bead spray with nine
4"-10" (10.2cm-25.4cm) strands

one package of gold Zingers bullion

four 10" (25.4cm) sprigs of dried
natural baby's breath

gold glitter spray

24-gauge white wire

hot glue gun and sticks

1. Measure the headband around the maid's head and form into a circle of a comfortable size; wrap the ends over each other to secure. Glue one end of the 1/4" (.6cm) wide ribbon near the beginning of the beaded area of the headband; wrap the ribbon spiral fashion around the wires to conceal them, gluing the end to secure. (This area will rest on one side of the maid's head.)

2. Use the tulle to make a puffy bow with four 4½" (11.4cm) loops and three 9"-11" (22.9cm-27.9cm) tails. Glue to the center of the empty area on the headband. Use the lace ribbon to make a puffy bow with two 3" (7.6cm) loops and 8"-9" (20.3cm-22.9cm) tails; glue it to the tulle bow center.

3. Glue the begonia leaf to the bow center, extending downward and right; glue the begonia blossoms over the leaf. Cut one 4-blossom chickweed sprig to 5" (12.7cm) and glue it under the lowest begonia blossom. Cut the remaining chickweed sprigs to 2½" (6.4cm) and glue, evenly spaced, around the begonias. Glue the daisy sprigs, evenly spaced, around the begonias.

4. Cut the pearl spray apart; glue five 4"-6" (10.2cm-15.2cm) strands around the upper begonia blossom to extend outward. Glue four 7"-10" (17.8cm-25.4cm) strands to extend downward from under the longer flowers.

5. Cut a 4" (10.2cm) length of bullion and stretch it out to 5'-6' (152.4cm-182.9cm). Secure one end around the headband under the tulle bow; wrap spiral fashion around the headband once each way, securing the end by twisting the wires together. Cut a 5" (12.7cm) bullion length, stretch it to 4' (121.9cm) and form into five 3"-8" (7.6cm-20.3cm) loops; twist the ends to secure the loops, and then glue under the flowers to extend downward. Cut a 4" (10.2cm) bullion length, stretch it to 3' (91.4cm) and form into five 3" (7.6cm) loops. Glue these loops between the begonias to extend around the flowers.

6. Cut the baby's breath into 3"-6" (7.6cm-15.2cm) sprigs and glue, evenly spaced, around the chickweed sprigs of similar lengths. Spray the piece with gold glitter.

MAID'S SATIN HAT

M A I D ' S   S A T I N   H A T

2 stems of white silk flowers,
each with six 6"-12" (15.2cm-30.5cm)
strands of ½" (1.3cm) wide flowers

cream satin bridal hat

2¼ yards (205.7cm) of 1½" (3.8cm) wide
white wired ribbon

2¼ yards (205.7cm) of 1" (2.5cm) wide
pink/white wire-edged ribbon

6 yards (548.6cm) of 8" (20.3cm) wide white tulle

four 4" (10.2cm) long pearl/bead leaves

six pearl loop sprays,
each with three 1" (2.5cm) wide loops

four to five stems of rosario alstroemeria

white floral tape

low-temperature glue gun and sticks

1. Glue a silk flower stem to the hat crown so the strands extend over the brim back.

2. Measure 26" (66cm) from one end of the white ribbon; glue this spot over the stem at the crown. Loop the ribbon around the crown, gluing every 4" to 5"(10.2cm-12.7cm). Cross the end over the stem; let 32" (81.3cm) extend below the brim.

3. Repeat step 2 with the pink/white ribbon, leaving 24" (61cm) and 30" (76.2cm) tails; coil the ribbon around the crown as it is glued.

4. Cut the tulle into equal lengths. Pinch 18" (45.7cm) from one end and glue over the ribbons at the crown back. Loop, pinch and glue as for the ribbon. Form the tail into three 5"-7" (12.7cm-17.8cm) loops. Pinch the loop ends together and twist; glue the twisted ends at the crown back. Fold the remaining tulle length to make 32" (81.3cm) and 46" (116.8cm) tails. Pinch and twist the folded area, then glue to the hat under the bow and over the ribbons.

5. Cut the second silk flower stem apart. Glue sprigs among the bow loops to extend over the tulle. Glue the beaded leaves and pearl loops around the bow.

6. Cut the alstroemeria blossoms off the stem. Glue a cluster of three 3" (7.6cm) blossoms right of the crown center front; glue three 3" (7.6cm) blossoms left of the center front. Glue fourteen blossoms among the tulle and pearls at the crown back.

BRIDE'S ROSE HEADBAND

BRIDE'S ROSE HEADBAND

one braided pearl/bead headband

3¾ yards of 6" (15.2cm) wide white tulle

four stems of bridal pink roses

six 4" (10.2cm) long iridescent white silk fern leaves

six pearl sprays, each with three 1" (2.5cm) wide loops

26-gauge white wire

hot glue pan and pellets

1. Shorten the headband to fit the bride; wire the ends together. Use the tulle to make a puffy bow with nine 4½"-7" (11.4cm-17.8cm) loops; glue to the headband back.

2. Hold the ferns and pearls together; twist the wire stems together and trim the stems to 1" (2.5cm). Glue to the headband back as shown.

3. Cut the roses to 3"-3½" (7.6cm-8.9cm); glue in a cluster next to the bow.

Designer Tip:
Fresh flowers can be added to any headpiece. Warm them to room temperature, dip the stems into 220°F (104.4°C) pan glue and attach to the headpiece.

LACE HEADPIECE WITH FINGERTIP VEIL

LACE HEADPIECE WITH FINGERTIP VEIL

four 3" (7.6cm) long pearl/beaded leaves

3" (7.6cm) clear plastic hair comb

3 yards (274.3cm) of 45" (114.3cm) wide cream tulle

1²/₃ yards (152.4cm) of 2³/₄" (7cm) wide wire-edged lace ribbon

one cattleya orchid with yellow lip

white floral tape

18-gauge wire

glue pan and pellets at 220°F (104.4°C)

1. Wire the beaded leaves together, and then wire them to the comb so they extend forward. Spread them apart, making a cap.

2. Pinch one end of the tulle together and hold. Make an 11" (27.9cm) loop, bring the tulle back to the pinch and hold. Make a 14" (35.6cm) loop under the first loop, bring the tulle back and wire the pinched areas together, allowing the rest of the tulle to drape downward. Wire this pouf to the comb.

3. Use the lace ribbon to make a puffy bow with two 4" (10.2cm) and two 5" (12.7cm) loops, a 14" (35.6cm) tail and a 10" (25.4cm) tail. Glue the bow in front of the tulle loops. Glue the orchid to the bow, extending forward over the beaded leaves.

CANDLELIGHT BRIDE'S HEADPIECE

CANDLELIGHT BRIDE'S HEADPIECE

one beaded crown-style headpiece

one ivory silk rose stem with two 2 1/2" (6.4cm) wide roses, one bud and leaves

three pearl loop sprays, each with six 1 1/2"–4" (3.8cm–10.2cm) loops of five pearl beads

3 3/4 yards (342.9cm) of 54" (137.2cm) wide ivory tulle

3 1/3 yards (304.8cm) of 3/8" (1cm) wide ivory satin ribbon

one ivory silk magnolia stem with one 10" (25.4cm) wide blossom and 5 leaves

2 1/3 yards (213.4cm) of 2 1/4" (5.7cm) wide cocoa/gold organza ribbon

1 1/4 yards (114.3cm) of 1 1/4" (3.2cm) wide beige lace

three 24" (61cm) long brown pheasant feathers

one stem of flocked nuts with five 4" (10.2cm) sprigs of two to three 3/4" (1.9cm) wide nuts and brown silk leaves

1/2 ounce (14.2g) sage green dried Avena

four stems of natural dried Lagurus (bunny tails)

one 2 1/2" (6.4cm) long clear plastic comb

green florist tape

needle and ivory thread

copper spray paint

22-gauge wire

low-temperature glue gun and sticks

1. Spray the headpiece, roses and pearl loops very lightly with copper paint; let dry. Cut 86" (218.4cm) of tulle; fold down 37" (94cm). Cut 49" (124.5cm) of tulle; fold down 20" (50.8cm) and place over the first piece, with the folded edges even. Measure 8" (20.3cm) down from the folds and gather to 4" (10.2cm) wide; wrap with wire and stitch to hold. Glue 12" (30.5cm) of satin ribbon over the wire. Sew the veil to the back of the headpiece just above the satin ribbon.

2. Pull the leaves and six magnolia petals from the stem. Layer the loose petals around each other to form a bud; wire and wrap with tape. Cut the blossom stem to 2" (5.1cm) and rewrap with tape. Glue four leaves, the blossom and the bud over the satin ribbon as shown.

3. With the organza ribbon, make a collar bow with two 6" (15.2cm) loops, a 23" (58.4cm) tail and a 25" (63.5cm) tail; glue between the flowers as shown. From the lace ribbon, make a 6" (15.2cm) loop with a 26" (66cm) tail; secure with wire. Cut 20" (50.8cm), 24" (61cm), 27" (68.6cm) and 29" (73.7cm) lengths of satin ribbon; knot each 1/2" (1.3cm) from one end, and again 2" (5.1cm) from the first knot. Glue the other ends and the lace loop to the organza bow center. Cut the rose stems to 1" (2.5cm), the rosebud to 2" (5.1cm) and the leaves off the stem; glue in a cluster between the magnolias.

4. Cut an 11" (27.9cm), a 12" (30.5cm) and a 13" (33cm) feather tip. Glue to extend downward at an angle as shown. Cut 5" (12.7cm) and 6" (15.2cm) feather ends; trim the cut ends at an angle and glue under the magnolia blossom angling up and left. Cut the nut stem into five 4" (10.2cm) sprigs and the Avena into 3"–6" (7.6cm–15.2cm) sprigs; glue, evenly spaced, among the flowers. Glue the pearl loops and the Lagurus around the bow. Glue the comb inside the veil over the ribbon.

Floral Decorations

DECORATED SHOES & WRIST CORSAGE

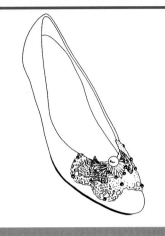

DECORATED SHOES

two 4" (10.2cm) round cream crocheted doilies

white shoes

two 2" x 1" (5.1cm x 2.5cm) bow-shaped brass charms

cotton swab, black acrylic paint, paper towels, gloss acrylic spray sealer (to antique charms)

two white fan motifs cut from embroidered trim

two ³/8" (1cm) round flat-backed pearl buttons, each with a shank

4" (10.2cm) strand of 3mm strung pearls

gold acrylic paint

soft paintbrush

paper towels

fabric glue

Goop glue

wire cutters

needle-nose pliers

For each shoe:
1. Measure 2¼" (5.7cm) from one edge of a doily; cut across the doily at this point, discarding the smaller piece. Position the doily over the shoe toe, folding under the cut edge; secure with fabric glue.

2. Antique and seal the charms. Gently bend one charm to fit over the shoe; use Goop to attach. Glue one fan over the charm center. Cut the shank from the button and glue the button over the fan.

3. Brush gold paint over the pearl length, then wipe off with a paper towel; let dry. Remove the pearls from the string. Use fabric glue to attach nine pearls around the doily edge and four around the fan edge.

WRIST CORSAGE

white plastic wrist corsage base

4" (10.2cm) round cream crocheted doily

two 2" (5.1cm) wide mauve silk begonia blossoms, each with a 3" (7.6cm) leaf

1 yard (91.4cm) of 1" (2.5cm) wide mauve/green wire-edged ribbon

1" (2.5cm) wide brass heart charm

cotton swab, black acrylic paint, paper towels, gloss acrylic spray sealer (to antique the charm)

three 3" (7.6cm) white silk chickweed sprigs, each with two 1" (2.5cm) wide blossoms

eight 3" (7.6cm) long white silk daisy sprigs, each with three ½" (1.3cm) wide blossoms

2" (5.1cm) of gold Zingers bullion

¼ ounce (7.1g) natural dried baby's breath

30-gauge white wire

hot glue gun and sticks

1. Remove and discard lace, if any, from the wrist corsage base. Glue the doily to the base. Glue a leaf to extend past the doily edge, angled downward right. Glue the other leaf angled upward left. Glue a begonia over each leaf, angled in the same direction as the leaf.

2. Use the ribbon to make a puffy bow with a center loop, four 2" (5.1cm) loops and 4" (10.2cm) tails. Glue it between the blossoms, angled in the opposite direction. Antique and seal the heart charm. Glue the charm on one side of the center loop, and then glue a white chickweed blossom on the other side.

3. Glue a chickweed sprig to extend from under each begonia over the leaf. Glue three daisy sprigs around the upper chickweed sprig; glue three more extending from below the lower begonia to form a triangle. Glue a daisy sprig on each side of the bow. Stretch the bullion to 36" (91.4cm); form it into 1"-2" (2.5cm-5.1cm) loops, twisting the ends to secure. Glue into the bow center.

4. Cut the baby's breath into 2"-4" (5.1cm-10.2cm) sprigs and glue, evenly spaced, among all the flowers.

MOTHER'S CORSAGE

M O T H E R ' S   C O R S A G E

six pearl loop stems, each with a 1½" (3.8cm) long loop of 3mm white pearls

six 4" (10.2cm) long white silk daisy stems, each with three sprigs of three ½" (1.3cm) wide blossoms

eight 4" (10.2cm) mauve silk chickweed sprigs, each with two 1" (2.5cm) wide blossoms

three 3" (7.6cm) long green silk begonia leaves, each with a 3" (7.6cm) stem

three 2" (5.1cm) wide mauve silk begonia blossoms, each with a 3" (7.6cm) stem

1 yard (91.4cm) of ⅝" (1.6cm) wide white/gold embroidered ribbon

4" (10.2cm) round cream crocheted doily

1" (2.5cm) wide brass heart charm

cotton swab, black acrylic paint, paper towels, gloss acrylic spray sealer (to antique charm)

6" (15.2cm) of gold Zingers bullion

gold paint

soft paintbrush

paper towels

30-gauge white wire

green floral tape

hot glue gun and sticks

1. Brush gold paint over the pearl loops, then wipe with paper towels and let dry. Hold a daisy and a chickweed sprig with a pearl loop in front of a leaf. Place a begonia blossom in front of them, then another daisy sprig, chickweed sprig and pearl loop in front of it. Wrap the stems with floral tape to hold.

2. Hold a leaf behind the cluster below the begonia, angled right. Add another begonia in front of the stems, angled over the last leaf. Position a chickweed sprig on each side of it and a daisy sprig in front. Add another pearl loop in front, then wrap the stems twice with floral tape. Wrap the stems with wire; twist the ends to secure. Cut the stems to 1" (2.5cm), then wrap floral tape to the ends. Set this cluster aside.

3. Hold two daisy sprigs, a pearl loop and a chickweed sprig in front of a leaf. Position a begonia in front, then add a chickweed sprig on each side, a daisy sprig and a pearl loop in front. Wrap the stems with floral tape to hold, then wrap with wire. Wrap more floral tape over the wire.

4. Position the clusters end to end, overlapping the stems and positioning the lowest flowers on each so they touch. Wire, then wrap with floral tape. Use the ribbon to make a puffy bow with a center loop, six 1¾" (4.5cm) loops and 4" (10.2cm) tails. Glue the bow over the stems, angled left.

5. Pinch the doily center and wrap with wire ¼" (.6cm) from the center to make a rosette; glue to the stems just left of the bow. Antique and seal the charm. Glue the charm between the doily and bow, angled upward. Cut chickweed blossoms off the remaining stem and glue to cover any exposed stems. Cut the stem off a pearl loop and glue the loop just right of the bow.

6. Cut one 1" (2.5cm) and two 2" (5.1cm) bullion lengths. Stretch the 1" (2.5cm) to 18" (45.7cm) and form it into 1"-1½" (2.5cm-3.8cm) loops; twist the ends to secure, then glue in front of the charm. Stretch each 2" (5.1cm) bullion length to 36" (91.4cm) and form into 1"-2" (2.5cm-5.1cm) loops; secure. Glue one behind the upper and one behind the lower begonia.

BOUTONNIERE AND CORSAGE

For Each Boutonniere:

one 1¼" (3.2cm) wide white silk rosebud

one 2½" (6.4cm) long
white dried baby's breath sprig

1¾" (4.5cm) wide silk ivy leaf
with a 1" (2.5cm) long stem

3" (7.6cm) of 26-gauge wire

green floral tape

corsage pin

pencil

basic supplies (see page 6)

For Each Corsage:

9" (22.9cm) of 1½" (3.8cm) wide ivory gathered lace

one 2½" (6.4cm) wide white silk rose

three 1½" (3.8cm) wide silk ivy leaves

1 yard (91.4cm) of ⅛" (.3cm) wide ivory satin ribbon

⅞ yard (80cm) of ⅛" (.3cm) wide white satin ribbon

three 3" (7.6cm) long white pearl sprays

five 1" (2.5cm) sprigs of white dried baby's breath

corsage pin

6" (15.2cm) of 30-gauge wire

basic supplies (see page 6)

1. *Boutonniere*—Remove the bud from its stem and glue the wire in its place. Hold the baby's breath and the ivy sprig next to the bud. Beginning at the top of the wire stem, wrap all of the stems together with floral tape, twisting the wire stem while you wrap.

2. Wrap the wire stem spiral fashion around a pencil to form a tendril. Insert the corsage pin into the tendril.

3. *Corsage*—Bend a tip of the wire over ½" (1.3cm) and thread the other end through the bound edge of the lace. Pull the lace tightly to gather, twist the wire ends together and trim. Glue the rose to the center of the lace circle. Glue the leaves under the rose but over the lace.

4. Hold the ribbons together and make a loopy bow with six 1½" (3.8cm) loops and 3" (7.6cm) tails. Glue over the center leaf. Glue the pearl sprays to the bow center. Glue the baby's breath over the ivy leaves, and insert the corsage pin through the lace in the back.

CANDLELIGHT BOUTONNIERE & MOTHER'S CORSAGE

BOUTONNIERE

one 1" (2.5cm) wide ivory silk rosebud
with two leaves on a 4" (10.2cm) stem

one 7" (17.8cm) long brown pheasant feather

one 4" (10.2cm) flocked nut sprig with two
½"–¾" (1.3cm–1.9cm) nuts and three brown silk leaves

one 2½" (6.4cm) wide ivory silk rose on a 3" (7.6cm) stem

three 2" (5.1cm) sprigs of sage green Avena

copper spray paint

green floral tape

22-gauge wire

low-temperature glue gun and sticks

MOTHER'S CORSAGE

five ¾" (1.9cm) wide ivory silk rosebuds and leaves
with 1" (2.5cm), 2½" (6.4cm), 3½" (8.9cm),
4" (10.2cm) and 5" (12.7cm) stems

two 2½" (6.4cm) wide ivory silk rose blossoms on
3" (7.6cm) and 4" (10.2cm) stems

one 7" (17.8cm) round ecru crocheted doily

¾ yards (68.6cm) of 1½" (3.8cm) wide
gold-dotted ivory satin ribbon

1 yard (91.4cm) of ⅞" (2.2cm) wide toffee satin ribbon

three 3" (7.6cm) green silk rose leaves

six 2" (5.1cm) sprigs of sage green dried Briza maxima
(quaking grass)

copper spray paint

green floral tape

22-gauge wire

low-temperature glue gun and sticks

For the Boutonniere:
Lightly paint the rosebud; let dry. Hold the feather, then lay the rosebud, nut sprig and rose over it (in that order). Wire the stems together and wrap twice with floral tape. Glue the Avena behind the rose.

For the Corsage:
1. Lightly paint the rosebuds; let dry. Hold, in a row, the 3½" (8.9cm), 4" (10.2cm), 5" (12.7cm) and 2½" (6.4cm) buds. Lay the 3" (7.6cm) and 4" (10.2cm) roses on top; wrap the stems once with wire and twice with florist tape.

2. Glue the backs of the corsage stems to the doily; fold the lower side edges of the doily in and glue to cover the upper stems. Leave the scalloped edges free as shown.

3. With the ivory ribbon, make a collar bow with 2½" (6.4cm) loops and 5" (12.7cm) tails. Glue at an angle near the blossoms, with one loop closer to the top rose. Glue one rose leaf and a rosebud angling downward and to the right from the bow center. From the toffee ribbon, make a puffy bow with a center loop, four 1½" (3.8cm) loops and 4" (10.2cm) tails; glue across the ivory bow center. Glue the rose leaves and Briza evenly among the flowers.

GARDEN RITES BOUTONNIERE & MOTHER'S CORSAGE

BOUTONNIERE

five 8"–9" (20.3cm–22.9cm) natural birch twigs

four 6"–7" (15.2cm–17.8cm) natural birch twigs

one 5" (12.7cm) sprig of creamy-white/pink silk
oncidium orchids with five
3/4"–1½" (1.9cm–3.8cm) wide blossoms

3" (7.6cm) of 3/8" (1cm) wide beige satin ribbon

one 1½" (3.8cm) wide burgundy gardenia blossom

two rose leaves, 2" (5.1cm) long

one sprig burgundy silk berries

one ivy sprig with three leaves

22-gauge wire

low-temperature glue gun and sticks

MOTHER'S CORSAGE

two stems of pink silk roses,
each with one 4" (10.2cm) wide rose and leaves

one stem of burgundy silk berries with
a 4½" (11.4cm) three-berry sprig and
a 9" (22.9cm) five-berry sprig

1 yard (91.4cm) of 1" (2.5cm) wide white chiffon ribbon

1 yard (91.4cm) of 3/8" (1cm) wide pink satin ribbon

burgundy silk gardenias: a 2" (5.1cm) sprig with
two 2" (5.1cm) wide blossoms and a 2" (5.1cm) sprig
with one 2" (5.1cm) wide blossom and one 1" (2.5cm) bud

eight 4" (10.2cm) sprigs of white silk daisies,
each with three ½" (1.3cm) wide blossoms

22-gauge wire

green floral tape

low-temperature glue gun and sticks

For the Boutonniere:
Bend the 8"–9" (20.3cm–22.9cm) twigs into loops. Hold the 6"–7" (15.2cm–17.8cm) twigs behind them; wire all the ends. Wire the orchids, rose leaves and berries over the twigs. Glue the ribbon around the wires. Glue the ivy leaves and the gardenia above the berries.

For the Mother's Corsage:
1. Cut a 5" (12.7cm) and a 3½" (8.9cm) rose sprig. Cut the berries into a 4½" (11.4cm) three-berry and a 7" (17.8cm) five-berry sprig. Wire the stems together with the 5" (12.7cm) rose and the 4½" (11.4cm) berry angling right and the others left. Wrap tape twice around the wire.

2. Using the chiffon ribbon, make a puffy bow with six 2" (5.1cm) loops and 3" (7.6cm) tails. Wire and glue it below and right of the lower rose. Using the satin ribbon, make a puffy bow with a center loop, six 1½" (3.8cm) loops and 3" (7.6cm) tails. Wire and glue it over the chiffon bow center.

3. Glue the two-blossom gardenia stem above the lower rose and the other gardenia stem to the lower left of it. Glue two small leaves above and two below the lower rose. Glue six daisy sprigs around the lower rose and two right of the upper rose. Wrap the lower stems with florist tape.

CANDLELIGHT CAKE TOP & CORSAGES

CAKE TOP

one 4" x 4" x 1½" (10.2cm x 10.2cm x 3.8cm) block of floral foam for silks

one 3½" (8.9cm) cake top base with an ivory lace collar

one 2½" (6.4cm) tall clear glass votive cup

one stem of ivory silk roses with two 2½" (6.4cm) wide roses, one bud and leaves

two brown/orange latex fruit picks, each with a 1½" (3.8cm) wide apple, a 1¼" (3.2cm) wide apple, seven berries and four leaves

two stems of ivory silk rosebuds, each with five ¾" (1.9cm) wide buds and leaves

2 yards (182.9cm) of ⅞" (2.2cm) wide toffee satin ribbon

½ yard (45.7cm) of 1¼" (3.2cm) wide beige lace ribbon

½ ounce (14.2g) sage green dried Briza maxima

one 2" (5.1cm) ivory votive candle

copper spray paint, green floral tape

22-gauge wire, Goop adhesive

low-temperature glue gun and sticks

CORSAGE

one brown/orange fruit pick with a 1½" (3.8cm) wide pomegranate, a 1" (2.5cm) wide russet pear, a 1" (2.5cm) wide green pear, 6 assorted ¼"–1" (.6cm–2.5cm) wide berries and leaves

one stem of ivory silk roses with an 8" (20.3cm) section of two 2½" (6.4cm) wide roses, one rosebud and leaves

brown floral tape, 22-gauge wire

For the top:
1. Cut the foam to fit inside the cake top; glue. With the Goop, glue the cup on the foam; let dry overnight. Cut the stem of ivory roses into two 2" (5.1cm) blossom sprigs and a 3" (7.6cm) bud sprig. Glue into the foam front as shown. Cut the leaf sprigs to 2" (5.1cm) and insert around the roses.

2. Cut the components from a fruit pick; glue around the roses, with the two largest fruits between and the leaves below the flowers. Very lightly spray the ¾" (1.9cm) rosebuds with paint; let dry. Cut five rosebuds to 2" (5.1cm); glue among the other roses following the crescent line. Cut five rosebuds to 1½" (3.8cm) and glue evenly around the empty back.

3. Cut six 11" (27.9cm) lengths of satin ribbon. Fold one in half; wrap with wire 2" (5.1cm) from the fold; trim the wire to 2" (5.1cm). Repeat for five more. Cut six 3" (7.6cm) lengths of lace. Wire each in the center; trim the wire to 2" (5.1cm). Glue a satin and a lace loop on each side of the front left rose and the others around the back. Cut the components from the other pick and glue around the back with leaves angled down. Glue 2"–3" (5.1cm–7.6cm) Briza sprigs evenly among the flowers. Put the candle in the cup.

For the Corsage:
Lay the roses over the fruit pick and trim the excess off each stem. Wrap the stems once with wire and twice with tape. Bend the lower rose and some leaves toward the stem to create a crescent shape.

CAKE TOP

3" (7.6cm) wide cake top form with foam
for silk and dried flowers

8" (20.3cm) round pencil-edge white tulle bouquet collar

one mauve/green silk begonia bush with
five 3" (7.6cm) wide blossoms,
seven 2" (5.1cm) wide blossoms
and numerous leaves

five stems of white silk chickweed, each with
four sprigs of three 1" (2.5cm) wide blossoms

three stems of white silk Scottish heather, each with
four branches of three 5"-9" (12.7cm-22.9cm) sprigs
with pelletlike blossoms

3 yards (274.3cm) of 1" (2.5cm) wide
mauve/green wire-edged ribbon

3 yards (274.3cm) of ³/₈" (1cm) wide
metallic gold mesh wired ribbon

1 ounce (28.4g) natural dried baby's breath

two 1¹/₂" (3.8cm) wide brass open heart charms

cotton swab, black acrylic paint, paper towels,
gloss acrylic spray sealer (to antique charms)

22-gauge wire (for bows)

18-gauge wire

green floral tape

3" (7.6cm) wired wood picks

hot glue gun and sticks

1. Remove the lace from the cake top form and discard. Remove the stitches to separate the tulle from the collar; discard the collar. Glue the tulle around the cake top form.

2. Cut a 2" (5.1cm) begonia blossom to 7" (17.8cm) long and insert it into the center of the foam. Cut the 3" (7.6cm) wide blossoms to 4½" (11.4cm) long; insert, evenly spaced, around the outside of the foam, extending outward parallel with the table. Cut the remaining begonia blossoms to 5½" (14cm); insert at 45° angles, evenly spaced, between the center and outer flowers.

3. Cut 4" (10.2cm) begonia leaf sprigs and insert among all the flowers to separate them. Cut each chickweed stem into four 7" (17.8cm) sprigs and insert them, evenly spaced, among all the flowers to extend outward at the same angle as the begonias.

4. Cut each heather stem into four 9" (22.9cm) branches of three sprigs; insert as for the chickweed sprigs, pulling the longer sprigs down into the flowers.

5. Cut the ribbons into seven 14" (35.6cm) lengths. Hold a gold length over a mauve length and make a collar bow with two 3" (7.6cm) loops of each ribbon and no tails. Wire the bow to a wood pick; repeat for six more bows. Insert the bows, evenly spaced, among the flowers.

6. Cut the baby's breath into 6"-8" (15.2cm-20.3cm) sprigs and insert them, evenly spaced, among the flowers. Antique and seal the heart charms. Glue each charm to a 6" (15.2cm) length of 18-gauge wire; insert one on each side of the center begonia.

7. Place the cake top on the upper cake layer. Make seven boutonnieres. Place two end to end on the left side of the lower cake layer and two on the ruffle at the lower front. Place three in the same manner on the right side of the lower layer.

CAKE TOP

C A K E   T O P

1½" x 2½" (3.8cm x 6.4cm) floral foam
for dried flowers

3¾" (9.5cm) wide cake top with a white sheer ruffle

1" (2.5cm) wide pearl/beaded headband (see step 1)

two 8" (20.3cm) long white paper rose picks, each
with three 1½" (3.8cm) wide blossoms, one 1" (2.5cm)
wide blossom, three ½" (1.3cm) wide open buds,
many 1"–1½" (2.5cm–3.8cm) long green leaves
and ⅛"–¼" (.3cm–.6cm) wide green and red berries

six 1½" (3.8cm) wide white paper rose blossoms,
each with one 1½" (3.8cm) long green leaf

1 ounce (28.4g) light green plumosus

1 ounce (28.4g) white dried baby's breath

three 1½" (3.8cm) wide pearl loop picks
with 4" (10.2cm) long picks

1⅓ yards (121.9cm) of 1/16" (.2cm) wide
white satin ribbon

½ yard (45.7cm) of 2.5mm white fused pearls

one 3" (7.6cm) long floral pick with wire

basic supplies (see page 6)

1. Cut the floral foam to fit inside the cake top and glue. Bend the headband into a circle and glue the ends into the foam.

2. Cut each rose pick to 7" (17.8cm) and glue one on each side of the headband. Spread the open buds to extend naturally, with the 1" (2.5cm) blossom to the left, one 1½" (3.8cm) blossom to its left and two below. Cut the 1½" (3.8cm) single blossom stems to 2" (5.1cm) long and glue three, evenly spaced, below each pick. Discard the rose leaves.

3. Cut the plumosus and baby's breath into 2"–6" (5.1cm–15.2cm) sprigs and glue them among the roses, filling empty spaces. Insert a pearl loop on each side of the open buds at what will be the front of the cake top. Cut the last loop stem to 2" (5.1cm) and glue it among the materials at the bottom front.

4. Use the ribbon to make a loopy bow with eight 1½" (3.8cm) loops, a 3" (7.6cm) tail and a 4" (10.2cm) tail. Use the pearls to make a loopy bow with two 1½" (3.8cm) loops and 4" (10.2cm) tails. Cut the floral pick to 2" (5.1cm) long and wire bows to it, with the pearl bow in the center of the ribbon bow. Insert the pick into the bottom right of the foam.

Designer Tip:
Place the cake top on the smallest tier of your wedding cake. You can use plumosus and baby's breath around the base of the cake instead of fresh flowers.

GARLAND

For Every 5' (152.4cm) of Garland:

7" (213.4cm) of green silk ivy garland with
1¹⁄₈"–2" (2.9cm–5.1cm) long leaves

eight 4" (10.2cm) wide ivory silk rose blossoms with
two 5" (12.7cm) long leaves

eight 2" (5.1cm) wide ivory silk rosebuds with two
5" (12.7cm) long leaves

six stems of white silk mini roses, each with three
5" (12.7cm) sprigs of three 1" (2.5cm) wide roses

6 ounces (170.1g) green preserved sprengeri

4 ounces (113.4g) preserved baby's breath

2½ yards (228.6cm) of 1½" (3.8cm) wide
ivory sheer striped ribbon

green floral tape

24-gauge paddle wire

one dark green chenille stem or
green cloth-covered wire

basic supplies (see page 6)

1. Cut a 5' (152.4cm) length of ivy garland, then cut the remaining garland into 3" (7.6cm) sprigs. Cut the rose blossom and rosebud stems to 4" (10.2cm). Cut the mini rose stems to 7" (17.8cm). Cut the leaves from the rose stems. Hold a rose blossom, a few of the leaves, a mini rose sprig, two to four 4" (10.2cm) sprigs of sprengeri and one to two baby's breath sprigs together and floral tape the stems. Make a total of eight clusters. Repeat using the rosebuds, for eight more clusters. Make fifteen filler clusters with an ivy sprig and 4" (10.2cm) sprigs of sprengeri and baby's breath.

2. At one end of the garland hold a rosebud cluster next to the garland. Wire the two together by wrapping the paddle wire from the base of the blossom to the ends of the stems. Do not cut the wire.

3. Wire a filler cluster directly under the blossom cluster. Next add a rose blossom cluster. Repeat using the three types of clusters in this order until you have used each cluster. As you add them, the clusters may fall slightly to one side, which gives the garland a more natural look.

4. Beginning 3" (7.6cm) from one end of the ribbon, glue next to the first rose blossom and loop and glue down the length of the garland. Cut the chenille stems into even lengths and use the pieces (or cloth-covered wire lengths) to wire the garland down a candelabra or along the edge of a cake table.

Designer Tip:
The garlands are easily removed. They can be taken to the reception site and placed on a guest table with votive cups.

BUFFET TABLE ARRANGEMENT

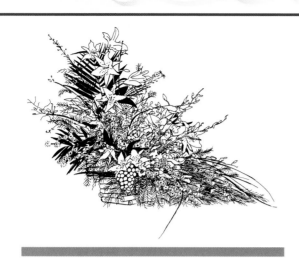

BUFFET TABLE ARRANGEMENT

floral foam (for fresh flowers) to fit each basket

plastic liner for each basket

one 8" (20.3cm) square log basket
decorated with moss

one 12" (30.5cm) square log basket
decorated with moss

six stems of stargazer lilies

three stems of emerald fern

twenty stems of bear grass

½ bunch of mingeri fern

fifteen stems of Dendrobium orchids

½ bunch of monte casino

1 pound (453.6g) of red grapes

leaf gloss spray

24-gauge wire

wood picks

hot glue gun and sticks

1. Soak the foam pieces and insert one into each liner. Place the liners into the baskets. Position the small basket with one corner overlapping a corner of the large basket (this will be the left side of the arrangement). Wire the baskets together and glue to prevent movement.

2. Insert a 27" (68.6cm) lily into the back of the upper basket, extending upright and establishing the height of the arrangement. Insert a 20" (50.8cm) lily horizontally into the right of the lower basket, establishing the width of the arrangement. Insert a 5" (12.7cm) lily stem horizontally into the left of the upper basket, establishing the third corner of the triangle. Use the remaining lily stems to fill the triangular area already established, spacing them evenly.

3. Insert an emerald fern stem behind the upper lilies; repeat behind the horizontal lilies on each side. This backs the lines of the design to give the arrangement depth.

4. Wire the bear grass stems to a wood pick at about 20" (50.8cm) and insert into the lower foam, extending right.

5. Insert the mingeri throughout the arrangement, adding depth.

6. Insert the orchids throughout the arrangement to fill the triangular shape, treating the two containers as one large container.

7. Insert the monte casino throughout the arrangement as with the orchids, making it light and airy.

8. Spray the grapes with leaf gloss; wire them to a wood pick. Insert the pick into the lower foam at the left so the grapes spill out over the edge of the container.

Designer Tip:
When working with a two-tiered arrangement, connect both tiers and treat them as if they were just one arrangement. This will give continuity, flow and balance o a large design.

RUNNER ARRANGEMENT WITH GARLAND

R U N N E R
A R R A N G E M E N T

8" × 5" × 2" (20.3cm × 12.7cm × 5.1cm) oval
plastic container

3½ yards (320cm) of 4½" (11.4cm) wide
eggshell flat lace ribbon

floral foam (for fresh flowers) to fit the container

one bunch of mingeri fern

eight stems of white Dendrobium orchids

3½ yards (320cm) of 2½" (6.4cm) wide
metallic gold mesh ribbon

four white Casablanca lily blossoms

basic supplies (see page 6)

G A R L A N D

three bunches of mingeri fern

30 yards (27.4m) of 4½" (11.4cm) wide
eggshell flat lace ribbon

25 yards (22.9m) of 2½" (6.4cm) wide
metallic gold mesh ribbon

spool wire

Runner Arrangement:

1. Wrap the container with ribbon, gluing to secure. Glue soaked foam into the container to extend 1" (2.5cm) above the rim. Insert 30" (76.2cm) fern stems into the foam front to extend forward. Insert 12"-24" (30.5cm-61cm) stems to extend upward, forward and to each side.

2. Cut 9"-15" (22.9cm-38.1cm) orchid stems; insert them into the front and top of the foam to extend forward and upward.

3. Make a puffy bow) with three 6" (15.2cm) loops, a 36" (91.4cm) tail and a 42" (106.7cm) tail; wire it to a wood pick and insert it into the front of the foam.

4. Cut the stems of all lilies to 4"(10.2cm). Insert one behind the bow and one in front of it. Insert one on each side, angled over the end of the container.

Garland:

1. Use spool wire to bundle three to four fern stems together. Do not cut the wire, but add more stems over the tops of the first, allowing the ends to hide the stems of the first bunch. Repeat to form a garland of the desired length.

2. Anchor one end of the garland under the runner arrangement and place it over the right edge of the fabric runner.

3. Tuck one end of the lace ribbon under the arrangement, then loosely loop it throughout the garland, tucking the ribbon among the greens every 8" to 10" (20.3cm-25.4cm) along the entire garland. Repeat with the gold ribbon.

FOR CENTER AND SIDE ARRANGEMENTS

gold Deco Lace spray paint

floral foam for silks

18-gauge wire

green floral tape

FloraLock stem adhesive

24-gauge white wire (for bows)

6" (15.2cm) wired wood picks

hot glue gun and sticks

FOR THE CENTER ARRANGEMENT

7" (17.8cm) tall ivory plastic ginger jar vase

6" (15.2cm) round cream crocheted doily

one mauve silk begonia plant with eleven 3" (7.6cm) and fourteen 2" (5.1cm) wide blossoms and leaves

2¼ yards (205.7cm) of 1½" (3.8cm) wide gold mesh ribbon

1½ yards (137.2cm) of ⅝" (1.6cm) wide white/gold embroidered ribbon

four stems of white silk heather, each with four feathery branches of three 4"-8" (10.2cm-20.3cm) sprigs

four stems of white silk chickweed, each with four 8" (20.3cm) sprigs of 1½" (3.8cm) wide blossoms

two packages of gold Zingers bullion

fifteen pearl drop sprays, each with five monofilament stems with one oval pearl on the end

FOR EACH SIDE ARRANGEMENT

3½" (8.9cm) tall ivory plastic footed bowl

6" (15.2cm) round cream crocheted doily

one white silk peony bush with five 4" (10.2cm) wide blossoms, three buds and many leaves

2¼ yards (205.7cm) of 1½" (3.8cm) wide gold mesh ribbon

1½ yards (137.2cm) of ⅝" (1.6cm) wide white/gold embroidered ribbon

three stems of mauve silk chickweed, each with four 8" (20.3cm) sprigs of 1½" (3.8cm) wide blossoms

eight 10" (25.4cm) sprigs of mauve silk impatiens, each with a cluster of 1½" (3.8cm) wide blossoms, buds and leaves

three stems of white silk daisies, each with three 10" (25.4cm) sprigs of thirty ½" (1.3cm) wide blossoms

1 ounce (28.4g) natural dried baby's breath

nine pearl drop sprays, each with five monofilament stems with one oval pearl on the end

one package of gold Zingers bullion

Lightly spray the vase and bowls gold; let dry. Glue doilies over the edges to extend 4" (10.2cm) down the ginger jar front and 3" (7.6cm) down the bowls. Glue foam into each container.

Center Arrangement:
1. Cut a 15" (38.1cm) begonia stem with a 3" (7.6cm) and two 2" (5.1cm) blossoms; insert upright into the center. Cut four 11" (27.9cm) stems with 3" (7.6cm) blossoms; insert these stems around the first one, angled slightly away. Cut five 9" (22.9cm) stems; insert these around the last ones at a 45° angle. Cut the rest into six sprigs, each with two 2" (5.1cm) blossoms. Insert these around the edge, parallel to the table.

2. Use the mesh ribbon to make a puffy bow with eight 3" (7.6cm) loops and 12" (30.5cm) tails. Use the white ribbon for a puffy bow with a center loop, eight 2" (5.1cm) loops and 10" (25.4cm) tails. Wire the white bow to the mesh bow, then wire both to a pick and insert into the center front.

3. Cut the heather branches off the stems; tape to 6" (15.2cm) lengths of 18-gauge wire. Cut one to 18" (45.7cm) and insert upright into the foam next to the longest begonia. Cut the rest to 10"-15" (25.4cm-38.1cm)

lengths; insert, evenly spaced, near flowers of similar lengths at similar angles. Cut, wire and insert the chickweed as for the heather, but without the 18" (45.7cm) stem.

4. Cut the bullion into 2" (5.1cm) lengths. Stretch one to 36"(91.4cm); form 3" to 4" (7.6cm-10.2cm) loops. Position a pearl spray over the loops and tape to a 6" (15.2cm) wire length. Repeat for twelve more stems. Insert three 15" (38.1cm) stems around the tallest begonia; cut and insert the rest among all the flowers. Make two more sets, but do not wire. Glue into the bow loops.

Each Side Arrangement:
1. Cut a peony stem to 8" (20.3cm); insert upright into the center. Cut the other blossoms and buds to 7" (17.8cm); insert the blossoms around the bowl edge, parallel to the table. Insert the buds around the upright stem at a 45° angle.

2. Make bows as in step 2; insert at the outer front. Cut 8"-9" (20.3cm-22.9cm) sprigs of chickweed, impatiens, daisies and baby's breath; insert, evenly spaced, among the peonies at similar angles.

3. Repeat step 4 to make nine 7"-8" (17.8cm-20.3cm) pearl/bullion stems. Insert, evenly spaced, among the flowers. Spray the foam with stem adhesive to secure the stems.

CRESCENT WATERFALL ALTAR ARRANGEMENT

CRESCENT WATERFALL ALTAR ARRANGEMENT

one 21" (53.3cm) Oasis racquet bar

seven 15" (38.1cm) white taper candles

seven plastic candle extender spikes for tapers

two bunches of mingeri fern

one bunch of bear grass

five stems of white Casablanca lilies

twelve stems of white Dendrobium orchids

twenty-five stems of white carnations

11½ yards (10.5m) of 4½" (11.4cm) wide eggshell flat lace ribbon

18½ yards (16.9m) of 2¾" (7cm) wide metallic gold mesh ribbon

basic supplies (see page 6)

1. Soak the Oasis racquet for half an hour. Insert the candles into the extenders at varying heights across the foam.

2. Insert 28"-36" (71.1cm-91.4cm) fern stems at the left, extending forward and out. Insert 36"-46" (91.4cm-116.8cm) fern stems at the right to extend downward. Layer the fern in, beginning with the longest and lowest branches.

3. Wire twenty-five bear grass strands together at the stems; repeat twice. Insert a cluster on each side and one to extend forward.

4. Cut a 28" (71.1cm) lily. Insert at the right to extend down; insert a 12" (30.5cm) stem above it. Cut an 18" (45.7cm) stem to insert into the left side. Insert two 12" (30.5cm) stems into the front, extending forward. Insert a 10" (25.4cm) stem in front.

5. Insert twelve 12"-16" (30.5cm-40.6cm) orchid stems around the candles to angle forward, upward and toward each side.

6. Insert twenty-five carnation stems near flowers of similar lengths, filling empty areas and extending the lines of the arrangement.

7. Cut two 2-yard (182.9cm) lace lengths. Fold each to make a 26" (66cm) and a 46" (116.8cm) tail. Wire each to a wood pick, then insert one into each end. Cut a 3-yard (274.3cm) length. Make an 18" (45.7cm) loop, one 22" (55.9cm) tail and one 42" (106.7cm) tail; wire to a pick and insert into the front. Use 2 yards (182.9cm) of lace to make a puffy bow with three 8" (20.3cm) loops and 12" (30.5cm) tails; wire to a pick and insert in front of the right candles.

8. Cut a 5-yard (457.2cm) gold ribbon length; make a 36" (91.4cm) loop with a 45" (114.3cm) tail and a 60" (152.4cm) tail. Wire to a pick and insert into the right end to cascade over the fern. Cut a 4-yard (365.8cm) ribbon length; make a 29" (73.7cm) loop with a 28" (71.1cm) tail and a 40" (101.6cm) tail. Wire to a pick and insert into the front. Fold a 2½ yard (228.6cm) ribbon length, making a 40" (101.6cm) and a 57" (144.8cm) tail; wire to a pick and insert into the left end.

9. Cut three 84" (213.4cm) gold ribbon lengths. Use each to make a puffy bow with four 7" (17.8cm) loops and 10" (25.4cm) tails. Wire each to a wood pick; insert one in front of the candle on the right, one in the front near the left end and one in the front near the right end.

PEW DECORATIONS

ELABORATE AND SIMPLE DECORATIONS

gold glitter spray

pew clips

24-gauge white wire

hot glue gun and glue

ELABORATE DECORATION

6 yards (548.6 cm) of 4" (10.2 cm) wide ivory tulle

6 yards (548.6 cm) of 6" (15.2 cm) wide white tulle

5 yards (457.2 cm) of ³/₈" (1 cm) wide
gold mesh wired ribbon

3½ yards (320 cm) of 1" (2.5 cm) wide
mauve/green wire-edged ribbon

3½ yards (320 cm) of 2³/₄" (7 cm) wide
ivory wire-edged lace ribbon

two stems of mauve silk begonias,
each with a 3" (7.6 cm) wide blossom and two leaves

one stem of mauve silk impatiens with two
6" (15.2 cm) sprigs of blossoms and leaves

¼ ounce (7.1 g) natural dried baby's breath

one stem of white silk chickweed with four
8" (20.3 cm) sprigs of 1½" (3.8 cm) wide blossoms

six white pearl drop sprays

SIMPLE DECORATION

7 yards (640 cm) of 4" (10.2 cm) wide ivory tulle

7 yards (640 cm) of 6" (15.2 cm) wide white tulle

3½ yards (320 cm) of ³/₈" (1 cm) wide
gold mesh wired ribbon

2½ yards (228.6 cm) of 1½" (3.8 cm) wide
mauve/green wire-edged ribbon

one stem of mauve silk begonias with one 3" (7.6 cm)
wide blossom and two leaves

two stems of natural dried baby's breath

For the Elaborate Decoration:

1. Hold the tulle lengths together and handle as one. Make a puffy bow with six 9" (22.9cm) loops, a 24" (61cm) loop and a 36" (91.4cm) tail.

2. Place the gold and mauve/green ribbons over the lace ribbon and handle as one. Make a puffy bow with four 5½" (14cm) loops. Before cutting the ribbons, make these tails and loops: a 33" (83.8cm) and a 36" (91.4cm) lace tail; a 20" (50.8cm) loop and a 26" (66cm) mauve/green tail; a 24" (61cm), a 36" (91.4cm) and two 29" (73.7cm) gold mesh tails. Glue this bow to the tulle bow center.

3. Cut the begonias to 3" (7.6cm); glue one angled upward and one downward from the bow center. Glue an impatiens sprig under the upper begonia, angled right; glue the other under the lower begonia, also angled right.

4. Cut three 6" (15.2cm) chickweed sprigs off the stem. Glue one in front of each impatiens sprig. Glue one to extend from between the begonias, angled right. Cut the last chickweed sprig into two 4" (10.2cm) sprigs; glue to extend from under the begonias on the left side.

5. Glue a 6" (15.2cm) pearl drop spray next to each impatiens sprig; glue two 4" (10.2cm) sprays around the begonias. Cut the baby's breath into 3"-7" (7.6cm-17.8cm) sprigs; glue them, evenly spaced, among all the flowers. Spray with gold glitter, then glue the pew clip to the back of the tulle bow.

For the Simple Decoration:

1. Hold the two tulle lengths together; make a puffy bow with six 8" (20.3cm) loops, two 33" (83.8cm) tails, one 36" (91.4cm) tail and one 44" (111.8cm) tail. Hold the gold ribbon over the mauve/green ribbon and make a puffy bow with four 4½" (11.4cm) loops. Before cutting the ribbon, make a 23" (58.4cm) loop from the mauve/green ribbon and a 22" (55.9cm) loop, a 23" (58.4cm) tail and a 27" (68.6cm) tail from the gold ribbon. Glue to the tulle bow center.

2. Cut the begonia to 2" (5.1cm) long; glue to the bow center. Cut 3"-5" (7.6cm-12.7cm) baby's breath sprigs; glue them, evenly spaced, around the begonia. Spray with gold glitter, then glue the pew clip to the back of the tulle bow.

PEW DECORATION

1. Insert the galax leaves, evenly spaced, around the foam sides to form a collar. Cut the lily stem to 8" (20.3cm) and insert upright into the foam. Cut 8"-15" (20.3cm-38.1cm) stems of fern; insert them around the lilies with the longer ones extending downward and the shorter ones extending to the top and sides.

2. Use the ribbon to make a puffy bow with eight 5" (12.7cm) loops and 46" (116.8cm) tails. Attach to a wood pick and insert into the foam left of the flowers.

3. Insert three 18" (45.7cm) orchid stems into the foam, angled right, one horizontally, one above and one below.

Designer Tip:
When designing pew decorations, it must be considered that they are viewed from three sides. Remember that they face each other on consecutive pews. When designing, it is imperative that the cascades all flow in the same direction.

PEW DECORATION

six galax leaves

one pew holder with foam for fresh flowers

one stem of Casablanca lilies

six stems of mingeri fern

4 yards (365.8 cm) of 4 1/2" (11.4 cm) wide eggshell flat lace ribbon

three stems of white Dendrobium orchids

4" (10.2 cm) long wood picks

1

2

3

4 (back view)

CANDLELIGHT PEW DECORATION

one stem of ivory silk rosebuds with five ¾" (1.9cm)
wide buds and leaves

one 3½" x 3¾" (8.9cm x 9.5cm) white plastic pew
cup with detachable handle (see step 1)

one 12" (30.5cm) round ecru crocheted doily

one 3½" (8.9cm) foam cage for silk flowers

one 2½" (6.4cm) tall clear glass votive cup

2¾ yards (251.5cm) of 6" (15.2cm) wide ivory tulle

2¾ yards (251.5cm) of 1½" (3.8cm) wide
beige/brown wired ribbon

one stem of ivory silk roses with two 2½" (6.4cm)
wide blossoms, one bud and leaves

one brown/orange latex fruit pick with a 1¼" (3.2cm)
wide pomegranate, a 1¼" (3.2cm) wide apple,
a 1¼" (3.2 cm) wide pear,
six ½"–1" (.3 cm–2.5 cm) berries and five leaves

¼ ounce (7.1g) green sheet moss

¼ ounce (7.1g) sage green dried Briza maxima

one 2" (5.1 cm) ivory votive candle

22-gauge wire

copper spray paint

needle and ivory thread

low-temperature glue gun and sticks

Goop adhesive

1. Very lightly spray the ¾" (1.9cm) rosebuds with paint.
Let dry. Glue the pew cup in the center of the doily. Bring
the doily edges inside the cup evenly and glue. Glue the
foam cage over the cup, building up glue around the
edges. Using Goop, glue the votive cup centered on the
foam. Let dry twenty-four hours.

2. Fold one yard of tulle in half lengthwise. With the
needle and thread, sew a running stitch near the folded
edge. Gather and glue the tulle around the base of the
votive cup. With 1¾ yards (160cm) of tulle, make a
puffy bow with two 5" (12.7cm) loops, an 8" (20.3cm)
loop and a 14" (35.6cm) tail. Glue to the foam in front,
left of center. With the brown ribbon, make a collar bow
with 3" (7.6cm) loops and one 12" (30.5cm) tail. Glue
over the tulle bow.

3. Cut the ivory roses and bud with a 2" (5.1cm) stem.
Glue one blossom into the foam center front, one 1"
(2.5cm) down on the right side, and the bud 2" (5.1cm) up
and on the left side. Glue their leaves around them. Cut the
components from the pick. Glue three berries angled down
from the bow center and the other fruits and berries evenly
spaced among the flowers; save the leaves.

4. Cut the copper rosebuds to 1" (2.5cm). Glue them, evenly
spaced, along the back of the foam. Glue leaves (from step 3)
evenly around the buds. Glue moss over any exposed foam.
Glue 2"–4" ((5.1cm–10.2cm) Briza sprigs, evenly spaced,
among all the flowers. Place the candle in the votive cup.

Note:
Remove the handle from the holder to use the piece
as a table decoration.

P E W   B O W

5 yards (457.2cm) of 6" (15.2cm) wide ivory tulle

5 yards (457.2cm) of 5" (12.7cm) wide
sheer striped ivory wire-edged ribbon

one 2½" (6.4cm) wide ivory silk opening rosebud with
a 24" (61cm) long stem and two 5" (12.7cm) long stems
of 1¾"–2" (4.5cm–5.1cm) long leaves

one 4" (10.2cm) wide ivory silk rose blossom with a
24" (61cm) long stem and two 5" (12.7cm) long sprigs
of 1¾"–2" (4.5cm–5.1cm) long leaves

green floral tape

two 10" (25.4cm) green silk ivy sprigs with
1"–2" (2.5cm–5.1cm) long leaves

two 8" (20.3cm) green silk ivy sprigs with
1"–2" (2.5cm–5.1cm) long leaves

one 4" (10.2cm) long pew bow holder

12" (30.5cm) long chenille stem or
24-gauge white cloth-covered wire

basic supplies (see page 6)

1. Use the tulle to make a loopy bow with six 6" (15.2cm) loops and 24" (61cm) long tails. Use the striped ribbon to make a puffy bow with a center loop, eight 5" (12.7cm) loops and 26" (66cm) long tails. Wire the tulle bow behind the striped bow.

2. Cut the rosebud stem to 14" (35.6cm) and the rose stem to 12" (30.5cm). Hold them together with the ends flush and floral tape them together. Repeat, holding a 10" (25.4cm) ivy sprig between the 8" (20.3cm) ivy sprigs. Floral tape them to the backs of the rose stems. Tape the remaining ivy sprig pointing down, then curve the ivy sprigs naturally.

3. Wire the bows 4½" (11.4cm) below the rose blossom so the single ivy stem extends down between the bow tails.

4. Wire each bow to the loop on the pew bow holder. Place a bow on every other pew. You can drape tulle or ribbon from pew to pew: Attach the tulle or ribbon to the hook at the bottom of each holder.

To drape tulle, measure the aisle and add half that length to the aisle measurement. For example, if the aisle is 50' (15.2m) long, use 75' (22.9m) of tulle.

The bows can be detached after the ceremony and placed on guest tables at the reception.

Accessories

WRIST GLOVE
BRIDE'S GARTER
GARTER
FAVORITE FAVOR IDEAS
HAT FAVORS
CLEAR PLASTIC FAVORS
DOILY FAVORS
EMBELLISHED BOX FAVORS
PARASOL
LARGE HEART FRAME
WEDDING ALBUM WITH INSIDE FRAME
TAPESTRY ALBUM
BRIDE'S PHOTO ALBUM
CAKE KNIFE, SERVER, TOASTING GLASSES
AND PICTURE FRAME
CANDLE DECORATION, BOUTONNIERE
AND CAKE KNIFE
UNITY CANDLE

WRIST GLOVE & BRIDE'S GARTER

WRIST GLOVE

two 11" x 4" (27.9cm x 10.2cm) white
triangular sequined appliqués
3" (7.6cm) of 3/4" (1.9cm) wide
white self-adhesive Velcro
basic supplies (see page 6)

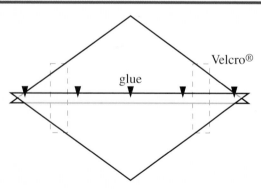

1. Place the appliqués as shown in the diagram and glue together at the arrows with small glue dots.

2. Measure around the bride's wrist and add 1" (2.5cm) for overlap. Cut equal amounts off each end of the joined piece to match this measurement. Press the soft section of the Velcro to the back of one end, parallel to the glove center. Trim the organza backing and Velcro to match the appliqué design. Repeat on the other end, but use the hook section of Velcro and adhere it to the front of the other glove end. Check to make sure the glove fits comfortably around the wrist before trimming.

BRIDE'S GARTER

2/3 yard (61cm) of 3 1/2" (8.9cm) wide white
garter lace (one side is 2" (5.1cm) wide
gathered double lace,
the other side 1" (2.5cm)
wide gathered single lace,
with 3/4" (1.9cm) wide flat
beading lace sewn over the join)
2/3 yard (61cm) of 1/4" (.6cm) wide elastic
small safety pin or bodkin (to thread the elastic
through the beading)
1 yard (91.4cm) of 1/8" (.3cm) wide white satin ribbon
three 3/4" (1.9cm) wide pink/white fabric roses
one white diamond/pearl spray with six 4" (10.2cm)
long sprigs
one white silk lily of the valley spray with four 4"
(10.2cm) long sprigs
basic supplies (see page 6)

1. Measure the bride's thigh and add 3" (7.6cm); cut the garter lace to this measurement. Subtract 3" (7.6cm) from the thigh measurement and cut the elastic to this measurement. Thread the elastic through the beading of the garter lace, being careful not to let the tail of the elastic slip inside. Overlap the lace/elastic ends 1/2" (1.3cm) and sew 1/8" (.3cm) from one end, stitching back and forth over the elastic to reinforce it. Repeat 1/8" (.3cm) from the other end.

2. Use the ribbon to make a loopy bow with six 1 1/2"–2 1/2" (3.8cm–6.4cm) loops and 4" (10.2cm) tails. Glue over the seam at the beading center. Cut the pearl and lily of the valley sprays to varying lengths and glue to the bow center, extending downward. Glue the roses in a cluster to the bow center.

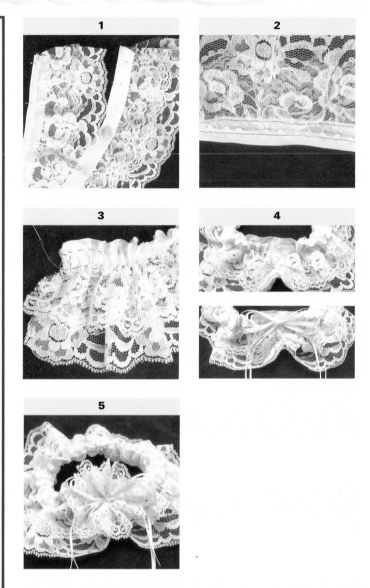

GARTER

15" (38.1cm) of 1/2" (1.3cm) wide white elastic

2/3 yard (61cm) of 2 1/2" (6.4cm) wide ivory gathered lace

2/3 yard (61cm) of 3 1/2" (8.9cm) wide ivory gathered lace

2/3 yard (61cm) of 7/8" (2.2cm) wide ivory satin ribbon

1 yard (91.4cm) of 1/8" (.3cm) wide ivory satin ribbon

1 yard (91.4cm) of 1/16" (.2cm) wide white satin ribbon

9" (22.9cm) of 1 1/2" (3.8cm) wide ivory gathered lace

three 3/8" (1cm) wide white pearl loops

one 1/4" (.6cm) wide safety pin

straight pins

needle and ivory thread

sewing machine

fabric glue

basic supplies (see page 6)

1. Measure the bride's thigh, subtract 3" (7.6cm) and cut the elastic to this length. Set aside for step 3. Lay the 2 1/2" (6.4cm) wide lace over the 3 1/2" (8.9cm) wide lace so the bindings are even. Pin the 7/8" (2.2cm) wide satin ribbon to the bindings, extending above the lace edge 3/16" (.5cm).

2. Sew a running stitch the length of the lace 1/8" (.3cm) from the bottom edge of the ribbon and another stitch 3/8" (1cm) from the top edge. (Use ivory thread; red thread was used to make the stitches visible in the photo.)

3. Insert the safety pin through one end of the elastic and thread it between the seams: Don't let the tail of the elastic slip inside. Spread the lace gathers evenly along the elastic. Doublestitch each of the ribbon/elastic ends 1/8" (.3cm) from the end.

4. Sew a running stitch on each raw edge of the 2 1/2" (6.4cm) and 3 1/2" (8.9cm) lace, and pull to gather. Use the machine to sew each gathered side together securely, overlapping slightly. Hold the remaining ribbon lengths together and make a loopy bow with six 2" (5.1cm) loops and 5" (12.7cm) tails. Glue the bow over the seam at the garter center.

5. Use the needle and thread to sew a running stitch through the bound edge of the 1 1/2" (3.8cm) wide lace. Pull the lace tightly to gather into a circle, knot the thread and trim. Glue the lace circle over the bow, then glue the pearl loops in the circle center as shown.

FAVORITE FAVOR IDEAS

HEART

2 1/2" (6.4cm) wide clear plastic heart
ten white Jordan almonds
9" (22.9cm) white tulle circle with gold edge
12" (30.5cm) of 5/8" (1.6cm) wide white ribbon
gold wire-edged ribbon

Fill the heart with almonds; place the heart in the center of the tulle. Gather the tulle edges around the heart. Use the ribbon to cinch the tulle in a shoestring bow with 1" (2.5cm) loops and 3" (7.6cm) tails.

BIRDSEED FAVOR

one 9" (22.9cm) white tulle circle with iridescent edge
one 9" (22.9cm) white lace circle
1/8 cup (56.7g) birdseed
two 12" (30.5cm) lengths of 1/16" (.2cm) wide white satin ribbon
8" (20.3cm) of 2mm white fused pearls
one 3/4" (1.9cm) wide white satin ribbon rose with green leaves
low-temperature glue gun and sticks, or tacky craft glue

Place the tulle over the lace circle; then pour the birdseed in the center of the tulle. Gather up the edges of the tulle and, holding both ribbon lengths together, tie a shoestring bow with 1" (2.5cm) loops and 3" (7.6cm) tails. Glue the center of the pearl length to the center of the bow. Knot the pearl tails 1/4" (.6cm) from each end and glue the ribbon rose to the bow center.

LACY ROSE SACHET

12" (30.5cm) of 4 3/4" (12.1 cm) wide white lace
12" (30.5cm) of 1 1/4" (3.2 cm) wide sheer white ribbon
sewing machine
white thread
1/4 cup (113.4g) dried rose petals

1. Fold the lace strip in half, wrong sides together, and sew a seam down each side 1/4" (.6cm) from the edges to form a bag. Fill with rose petals; use the ribbon to tie a shoestring bow with 1 1/4" (3.2cm) loops and 1 1/2" (3.8cm) tails 2" (5.1cm) from the top of the bag. The petals can be thrown, or the bag makes a fragrant sachet.

2. To dry your own rose petals, choose fresh, unblemished petals. Spread them out on newspapers in a warm, dry place for several days. Wait until they are completely dry to store them in a paper bag or shoe box, or they will mold.

Other Ideas:
Favors may be set at each guest place at the reception for a formal dinner, or passed out by the attendants or flower girls in a more casual setting.

Because of the mess, some churches and reception sites do not allow anything to be thrown by guests as the newlyweds leave. In that case, try one of these ideas.

• Give a small bell tied with pretty ribbons to each wedding guest as a keepsake to ring as the newlyweds leave.
• Pass out small bottles of bubbles for the guests to blow as the couple leaves. Be careful when using bubbles indoors, as floors can get slick; they are best used outdoors on pavement.

TOP HAT

two 9" (22.9 cm) circles of ivory tulle net

one 1" (2.5 cm) square of
groom's cake wrapped in gold foil

12" (30.5cm) of ⅛" (.3 cm) wide ivory satin ribbon

18" (45.7cm) of ⅝" (1.6 cm) wide ivory satin ribbon

one 3 ¼" x 2 ½" x 2" (8.3 cm x 6.4 cm x 5.1 cm)
black plastic top hat

IVORY HAT

15" (38.1 cm) of 6" (15.2 cm) wide ivory tulle net

12" (30.5 cm) of 4mm white fused pearls

3 ½" (8.9 cm) wide ivory crocheted hat

½ yard (45.7cm) of ⅞" (2.2 cm) wide
ivory satin ribbon

ten party mints

one 3" (7.6 cm) square of ivory tulle net

30-gauge wire

wire cutters

low-temperature glue gun and sticks,
or tacky craft glue

Photo inset is bottom view

1. Lay one tulle circle over the other and place the cake in the center. Gather the tulle around the cake. Wrap the ⅛" (.3cm) ribbon around the gathers just above the cake and tie in a shoestring bow with ¾" (1.9cm) loops and 1¾" (4.5cm) tails.

2. Wrap the ⅝" (1.6cm) satin ribbon around the crown of the hat and tie in a shoestring bow with ⅝" (1.6cm) loops and 1" (2.5cm) tails. Set the hat on its top and place the wrapped cake inside.

1. Twist the 15" (38.1cm) tulle length into a ½" (1.3cm) wide band. Hold the pearls 3" (7.6cm) from one end of the tulle and wrap them spiral fashion five times around the tulle. Wrap the tulle around the hat crown. Wire the ends together close to the crown.

2. Run a line of glue under the tulle band and wired ends to secure them to the hat. Trim the tulle tails to 3" (7.6cm) and the pearls to 1½" (3.8cm) long. Use the ribbon to make an oblong bow with a center loop, two 1⅝" (4.1cm) loops, two 1⅜" (3.5cm) loops and 2" (5.1cm) tails. Glue the bow over the wired area of the tulle.

3. Turn the hat over and fill with candy. Apply a line of glue around the opening, press the tulle square into it and let dry. Trim away excess tulle close to the glue line.

BOWL FAVOR

one 3" (7.6cm) round clear plastic bowl

fifteen candy mints

two 12" (30.5cm) circles of white tulle net

12" (30.5cm) of 1/4" (.6cm) wide metallic gold ribbon

one 1" (2.5cm) wide mauve silk rose

four 1" (2.5cm) sprigs of white glittered dried baby's breath

7/8" (2.2cm) wide brass double heart charm

low-temperature glue gun and sticks

HEART FAVOR

3 1/2" x 2" (8.9cm x 5.1cm) of white card stock (optional--see step 1)

12" (30.5cm) of 5/8" (1.6cm) wide pink satin ribbon

one 3" (7.6cm) wide clear plastic puffed heart

1/2 cup (226.8g) rose potpourri

two 12" (30.5cm) squares of white tulle net

one 1 1/2" (3.8cm) wide white silk rose

9" (22.9cm) of 4mm white fused pearls

1/4" (.6cm) wide hole punch

decorative edge scissors

low-temperature glue gun and sticks, or tacky craft glue

1. Fill the bowl with candy. Lay the tulle circles one over the other, place the bowl in the center and gather the tulle around the bowl. Wrap with the ribbon and tie in a shoestring bow with 1 1/4" (3.2cm) loops and 2" (5.1cm) tails.

2. Glue the rose to the bow center. Glue the baby's breath sprigs around the rose. Glue the charm below and left of the rose.

We thank you for sharing this special day!

1. Have the message "Thank you for sharing this special day!" printed on the card stock (or photocopy the message at left) and trim the edges with the decorative scissors. Punch a hole 1/4" (.6cm) from the left edge and thread onto the ribbon.

2. Fill the heart with potpourri. Lay the tulle squares one over the other, place the heart in the center and gather the tulle around the heart. Wrap the ribbon around the tulle and tie a shoestring bow with 1 1/2" (3.8cm) loops and 1 1/2" (3.8cm) tails; slide the card to hang just to the right of the bow. Trim the tulle 2" (5.1cm) above the ribbon.

3. Glue the rose to the center of the bow. Cut the pearls into one 4" (10.2cm) and one 5" (12.7cm) length. Glue the ends of each together to make a loop. Glue the large loop below left of the rose and the small loop inside the large one.

TUBE FAVOR

¼ cup (113.4g) birdseed or rice

5" x 4" (12.7cm x 10.2cm) of ivory tulle net

4" (10.2cm) of ¼" (.6cm) wide white flat braid

4" (10.2cm) of 5" (12.7cm) wide ivory flat lace
with scalloped edges

12" (30.5cm) of ¼" (.6cm) wide gold metallic ribbon

30-gauge wire

wire cutters

low-temperature glue gun and sticks,
or tacky craft glue

LACE POUF

⅛ cup (56.7g) birdseed or rice

one 6" (15.2cm) round white fabric doily
with a 2" (5.1cm) wide crocheted lace edge

12" (30.5cm) of ⅜" (1cm) wide white taffeta ribbon
with gold-wire edges

one 1" (2.5cm) long brass cherub charm

low-temperature glue gun and sticks,
or tacky craft glue

1. Place the seed or rice in a 1" x 2½" (2.5cm x 6.4cm) mound on the center of the tulle. Fold the tulle snugly around the filler, overlapping the long edges 1" (2.5cm). Glue the seam closed. Wrap each end with wire to close; twist the wire ends tightly and trim the ends.

2. Glue the white braid diagonally across the lace piece. Lay the lace with the braid side down, place the favor on it at right angles to the scalloped edges and wrap the lace around the favor; use only a dot of glue to close the seam. Cut the ribbon into two 6" (15.2cm) lengths. Use one length to tie each end of the favor, wrapping it 1" (2.5cm) from the scalloped edge of the lace and making a shoestring bow with ⅝" (1.6cm) loops and ⅝" (1.6cm) tails.

Place the seed or rice in the doily center. Gather the doily around the filler. Wrap the ribbon around the doily above the filler and tie in a shoestring bow with 1" (2.5cm) loops and 1¼" (3.2cm) tails. Glue the charm below the bow center.

EMBELLISHED BOX FAVORS

SATIN HEART BOX

one 2¼" (5.7cm) wide white satin heart box

8" (20.3cm) of ⅜" (1cm) wide
white heart appliqué trim

18" (45.7cm) of ⅛" (.3cm) wide white satin ribbon

three ½" (1.3cm) wide mauve ribbon roses
with green leaves

four 1" (2.5cm) long sprigs of white glittered
dried baby's breath

ten candy mints (or desired candy for box)

30-gauge wire

wire cutters

low-temperature glue gun and sticks,
or tacky craft glue

top view

GOLD PEDESTAL BOX

three 1" (2.5cm) wide mauve silk roses

3½" x 1⅝" x 1½" (8.9cm x 4.1cm x 3.8cm) tall
gold/clear plastic box with a pedestal base

six 1" (2.5cm) sprigs of white glittered
dried baby's breath

6" (15.2cm) of 4mm white fused pearls

ten candy mints

low-temperature glue gun and sticks,
or tacky craft glue

1. Remove the box lid. Glue trim around the box bottom just below the lid edge, then replace the lid. Use the ribbon to make a loopy bow with eight 1" (2.5cm) loops and 1¼" (3.2cm) tails. Glue the bow to the center top of the lid.

2. Glue the roses in a cluster to the bow center and glue the baby's breath evenly spaced around the roses as shown. Fill the box with the candy.

1. Glue the roses in a cluster to the center top of the box lid. Glue the baby's breath in three clusters evenly spaced among the roses.

2. Cut the pearls into three 2" (5.1cm) lengths and glue the ends of each length together to make a loop. Glue a loop below each baby's breath cluster. Fill the box with the candy.

PARASOL

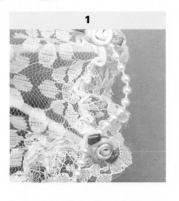

PARASOL

21" (53.3cm) of 4mm white fused pearls

one 6" x 6" (15.2cm x 15.2cm) white lace parasol

fourteen ½" (1.3cm) wide pink ribbon roses
with green leaves

two 1" (2.5cm) wide white chiffon blossoms

six 1" (2.5cm) sprigs of white glittered
dried baby's breath

low-temperature glue gun and sticks,
or tacky craft glue

1. Cut two 1½" (3.8cm) pearl lengths and set aside for step 3. Open the parasol. Loop and glue the remaining pearls in scallops between the ribs. Glue a pink rose to the end of each rib.

2. Glue a chiffon blossom to the handle base, with three roses around it.

3. Glue the second chiffon blossom to the parasol top, with the remaining roses evenly spaced around it. Glue the ends of each pearl length from step 1 together to form a loop. Glue a loop on each side of the chiffon blossom. Glue three baby's breath sprigs around the top and the rest around the handle cluster as shown in the large photo.

LARGE HEART FRAME

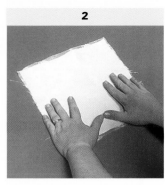

LARGE HEART FRAME

22" x 28" (55.9cm x 71.1cm) piece of posterboard

⅓ yard (30.5cm) of 45" (114.3cm) wide
white satin fabric

⅓ yard (30.5cm) of 45" (114.3cm) wide
white lace fabric

1" x 20" (2.5cm x 50.8cm) of 6–8 ounce
(170.1g–226.8g) polyester batting

5" (12.7cm) of ¼" (.6cm) wide white ribbon

⅔ yard (61cm) of 2" (5.1cm) wide white gathered lace

⅔ yard (61cm) of 1" (2.5cm) wide white gathered lace

1 yard (91.4cm) of ½" (1.3cm) wide
white satin gimp braid

⅔ yard (61cm) of ½" (1.3cm) wide
scalloped lace trim

1 yard (91.4cm) of 4mm white fused pearls

one 7" (17.8cm) long white pearl/flower

spray with one 2" (5.1cm) wide satin/organza
rose and a 1" (2.5cm) long rosebud

tracing paper

pencil

tacky board

spray glitter

spray adhesive

basic supplies (see page 6)

1. Trace the large heart, the large stand and the small stand patterns from page 128. Cut three large hearts, one large stand and one small stand from posterboard. Cut out and discard the inner heart from one heart. Cut one 6" x 9" (15.2cm x 22.9cm) piece, one 5" (12.7cm) square and three 10" (25.4cm) squares of satin. Repeat with lace.

2. Place the satin pieces right side up on the tacky board and smooth out wrinkles. Spray the satin pieces with adhesive and press the matching lace pieces over them (it is not necessary to align them perfectly). Remove the satin/lace sections from the board and set aside.

3. Place the two solid hearts and the stand posterboard pieces on the tacky board and spray with adhesive. Press a satin/lace square onto each heart, the 6" x 9" (15.2cm x 22.9cm) rectangle onto the large stand and the 5" (12.7cm) square onto the small stand. Remove from the tacky board and set aside.

4. Place the open heart on the tacky board and spray with adhesive. Press the batting strip onto the heart and trim the excess. Spray the batting, then press the remaining satin/lace square onto the front.

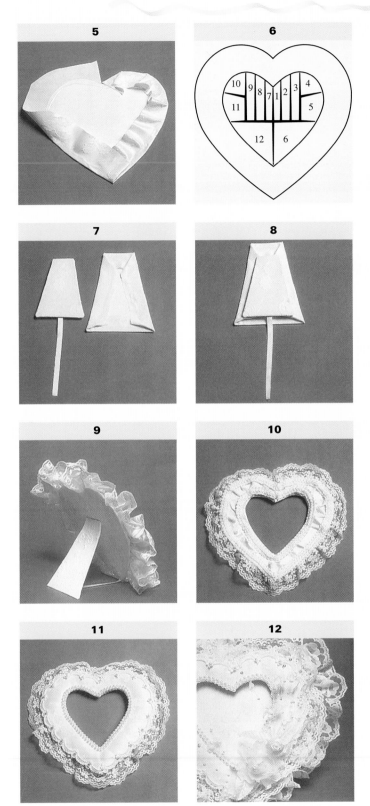

5. Trim the fabric 1½" (3.8cm) outside the edge of each heart. Cut the fabric to the center top point. Working from the slit down, a quarter section at a time, glue the fabric to the frame back, pleating out the excess.

6. *Open heart center*—Follow the diagram to cut slits in the inner fabric to 1/16" (.2cm) from the inner frame edge. If necessary, tuck the batting under. Glue the fabric sections to the back in numerical order, crossing sections 1 and 7 at the heart top. Trim excess fabric.

7. *Stand*—Trim the fabric to 1" (2.5cm) outside the edge of each piece. Glue the top edge down and the bottom edge up. Fold the bottom corners up diagonally and glue. Repeat with the top corners, then glue the sides. Glue the ribbon to the bottom back of the small stand piece as shown.

8. Glue the small stand to the large stand 1" (2.5cm) below the top edge.

9. *Frame back*—Glue 2" (5.1cm) lace to the back of one solid heart. Generously glue the other solid heart to the first, wrong sides together, and press firmly to avoid gaps. Place the stand on the center back, aligning the lower edges, and glue the top 1" (2.5cm) of the larger stand to the heart. Glue the ribbon end to the bottom back, adjusting the stand to hold the frame as desired.

10. Frame front: Glue 1" (2.5cm) lace to the back of the open heart. Glue gimp to cover the bound lace edge; glue another row of gimp around the inner heart edge.

11. Glue the scalloped trim around the outer edge of the heart front. Glue two rows of pearl trim around the inner edge. Cut individual pearls and glue one to the point of each scallop.

12. *Finishing*—Glue the frame front to the back from the bottom point to just above the widest part, leaving the top open to insert a photo. Bend the stem of the spray up and glue the spray to the lower right heart. Spray the frame with glitter.

WEDDING ALBUM WITH INSIDE FRAME

12" x 10" x 2½" (30.5cm x 25.4cm x 6.4cm) three-ring binder album

½ yard (45.7cm) of 6–8 ounce (170.1g–226.8g) polyester batting

1 yard (91.4cm) of 45" (114.3cm) wide white satin fabric

1 yard (91.4cm) of 45" (114.3cm) wide white lace fabric

table knife or screwdriver

1²/₃ yards (152.4cm) of 2" (5.1cm) wide white gathered double lace

2½ yards (228.6cm) of ½" (1.3cm) wide white satin gimp braid

tracing paper, pencil

basic supplies (see page 6)

HEART FRAME

8" (20.3cm) square of posterboard

10" (25.4cm) square of 45" (114.3cm) wide white satin fabric

10" (25.4cm) square of 45" (114.3cm) wide white lace fabric

1" x 20" (2.5cm x 50.8cm) of 6–8 ounce (170.1g–226.8g) polyester batting

²/₃ yard (61cm) of 2" (5.1cm) wide white gathered double lace

1 yard (91.4cm) of ½" (1.3cm) wide white satin gimp braid

²/₃ yard (61cm) of ½" (1.3cm) wide scalloped appliqué trim

1 yard (91.4cm) of 4mm white fused pearls

one 7" (17.8cm) long white pearl/flower spray with one 2" (5.1cm) wide satin/organza rose and a 1" (2.5cm) long rosebud

INSIDE FRAME

7½" x 9" (19.1cm x 22.9cm) of white satin fabric

7½" x 9" (19.1cm x 22.9cm) of white lace fabric

6" x 8" (15.2cm x 20.3cm) piece of posterboard

1" x 24" (2.5cm x 61cm) of 6–8 ounce (170.1g–226.8g) polyester batting

³/₄ yard (68.6cm) of 1" (22.9cm) wide white gathered lace

½ yard (45.7cm) of ½" (1.3cm) wide white satin gimp braid

½ yard (45.7cm) of ½" (1.3cm) wide scalloped appliqué trim

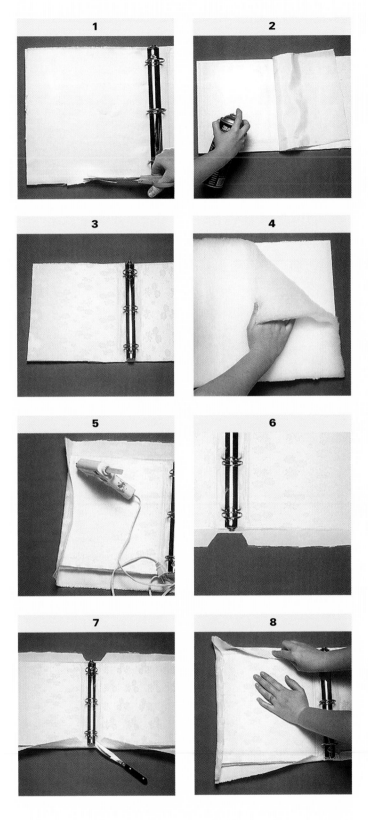

1. Remove and set aside the album filler pages. Open the album flat on the batting and cut the batting to fit. Repeat with the satin, but cut the satin 1½" (3.8cm) larger all around. Place one edge of the remaining satin against the binder on the inside of the album and cut to fit the front as shown; repeat for the back. Use the satin pieces as patterns to cut lace pieces. Follow page 100, step 2, to adhere the lace to the satin.

2. Use the glue gun to attach the satin/lace to the inside front next to the binder rings. Turn the fabric out of the way over the binder rings and spray the inside front with adhesive.

3. Smooth the fabric into place over the adhesive. Trim off any fabric that extends past the album edge. Repeat on the inside back.

4. Turn the album inside down. Use spray adhesive to adhere the batting to the front, spine and back; trim any excess.

5. Lay the large satin/lace piece right side down and center the album (batting side down) on it. Apply a bead of glue ½" (1.3cm) inside the front edge of the album and fold the fabric over, pressing it smoothly into the glue. Glue to secure the fold above and below the corners. Trim excess fabric. Repeat for the back edge.

6. Cut a notch in the top and bottom edges of the fabric next to the metal binder spine, leaving 1" (2.5cm) of fabric above and below the spine.

7. Glue the notched areas inside the album, using the table knife to press the notches under the metal.

8. Fold and glue the remaining edges as for the front and back edges, completing and trimming one section before beginning the next.

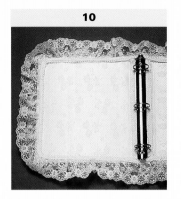

9. Beginning at the bottom right corner of the metal spine, glue the lace around the album edge. Pinch and glue the corners for extra fullness. Turn the album right side up and check that the lace is smooth and no binding shows; reshape if necessary.

10. Glue gimp to the album inside along each edge of the metal spine. Glue the remaining gimp to cover the bound edge of the lace. Use a damp washcloth to ease the gimp around the corners and curve it along the bottom and top of the spine.

11. Trace the large heart pattern from page 128 and cut one from posterboard. Cut out and discard the inner heart. Follow page 100, steps 2–4, and page 101, steps 5–6 and 10–11, to make the heart frame front, substituting double lace for the 1" (2.5cm) wide lace. Bend the stem of the spray up to conceal it and glue to the lower right heart. Glue to the album front, leaving the top 2" (5.1cm) unglued to insert a photo.

12. *Inside frame*—Place the satin fabric right side up on the tacky board and spray lightly with adhesive. Position the lace fabric right side up on the satin and smooth together; set aside. Measure and cut 1" (2.5cm) inside the edges of the posterboard piece; remove and discard the inner piece.

a. Place the posterboard frame on the tacky board and spray with adhesive. Cut the batting into one 4" (10.2cm), one 6" (15.2cm) and two 7" (17.8cm) lengths. Press to the frame front as shown in the diagram. Spray the batting with adhesive and press the satin/lace piece over the frame. Fold and glue the fabric to the back, folding in the corners diagonally.

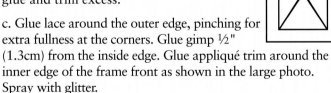

b. Cut across the fabric center in an X, stopping 1/16" (.2cm) short of the inner corners. Pull the sections to the frame back, glue and trim excess.

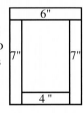

c. Glue lace around the outer edge, pinching for extra fullness at the corners. Glue gimp 1/2" (1.3cm) from the inside edge. Glue appliqué trim around the inner edge of the frame front as shown in the large photo. Spray with glitter.

d. Open the album, center the frame on the inside front cover and glue in place, leaving the top open to insert an invitation or photo. Spray the entire album with glitter.

TAPESTRY ALBUM

T A P E S T R Y   A L B U M

12" × 10" × 2½" (30.5 cm × 25.4 cm × 6.4 cm)
three-ring binder album

½ yard (45.7cm) of 6–8 ounce (170.1g–226.8g)
polyester batting

1 yard (91.4cm) of taupe tapestry fabric

2 yards (182.9cm) of ⅜" (1cm) wide
ivory rope piping with sew-in edging

2½ yards (228.6 cm) of ½" (1.3 cm) wide ivory satin
gimp braid

2 yards (182.9 cm) of 4mm
ivory fused pearls

table knife or screwdriver

spray adhesive

glue

basic supplies
(see page 6)

corner
cutting
diagram

1"

F R A M E

8" × 10" (20.3 cm × 25.4cm) photo mat

1½" × 25" (3.8 cm × 63.5 cm) of
2–4 ounce (56.7g–113.4 g) polyester batting

9½" × 12" (24.1 cm × 30.5 cm) of taupe tapestry fabric

⅔ yard (61 cm) of ½" (1.3 cm) wide
ivory satin gimp braid

1 yard (91.4cm) of ⅜" (1cm) wide
ivory rope piping with sew-in edging

1⅛ yards (102.9cm) of 4mm ivory fused pearls

¾ yard (68.6cm) of ⅝" (1.6cm) wide
ivory scalloped flat lace trim

one 3½" × 2¼" (8.9cm × 5.7cm)
ivory butterfly appliqué

one 6" × 2" (15.2cm × 5.1cm)
ivory floral appliqué

Follow pages 102-103, steps 1–10, to cover the album, using tapestry in place of the satin/lace and using piping in place of the lace trim. Glue pearls around the inner edge of the piping. Cut the corners off the mat as shown in the diagram below. Use spray adhesive to attach batting to the mat front; trim excess. Spray the batting with adhesive and press the tapestry onto it. Fold and glue the fabric to the back, folding in the corners. Cut across the fabric center in an X, stopping 1/16" (.2cm) short of the inner corners. Pull the sections to the frame back, glue and trim excess. On the back, glue gimp ½" (1.3cm) from the inside edge. Glue piping around the outer edge. On the front, glue pearls along the inner edge of the piping. Glue appliqué trim around the inside front, the butterfly to the top left and the floral appliqué to the lower right. Glue the frame to the album center front as shown, leaving the top open to insert a photo.

BRIDE'S PHOTO ALBUM

7¼" x 9¼" (18.4cm x 23.5cm) white photo album

two 6⅞" x 9" (17.5cm x 22.9cm) pieces of
white posterboard

white brocade fabric: one 18" x 10" (45.7cm x 25.4cm),
one 7½" x 5½" (19.1cm x 14cm),
and two 9½" x 7¾" (24.1cm x 19.7cm) pieces

2½ yards (228.6cm) of ⅝" (1.6cm) wide
white lace trim

5" x 7" (12.7cm x 17.8cm) white photo mat with
a 3" x 4½" (7.6cm x 11.4cm) opening

two 4¾" x 2" (12.1cm x 5.1cm) white appliqués
with pearls

spray adhesive

old newspapers

basic supplies (see page 6)

1. Place the album and posterboard pieces on the newspapers; spray the outside album cover and one side of each posterboard piece with adhesive. Smooth the 18" x 10" (45.7cm x 25.4cm) piece of fabric over the photo album. Repeat with the 9½" x 7¼" (24.1cm x 19.7cm) pieces over the sticky side of the posterboard pieces.

2. Fold the fabric sides over ½" (1.3cm) and glue inside the album. Miter the corners (see page 7). Fold the fabric under on the binding one more time.

3. Fold the top and bottom fabric edges over the posterboard pieces, then glue them to the back of the posterboard. Glue lace around the inside edges of the album, with the scallops extending out. Glue a posterboard piece inside the front and back covers.

4. Follow step 1 for the Picture Frame on page 107 to cover the mat with the 7½" x 5½" (19.1cm x 14cm) fabric piece. Glue the remaining lace around the inside and outside of the mat with the scallops extending out. Glue the appliqués to the mat as shown, then glue the mat to the album front. Leave the top edge open to insert the photo.

CAKE KNIFE, SERVER, TOASTING GLASSES & PICTURE FRAME

CAKE KNIFE, SERVER & TOASTING GLASSES

For Each Topper:

6" (15.2cm) of 1" (2.5cm) wide ivory gathered lace

12" (30.5cm) of 4mm ivory fused pearls

3⅓ yards (304.8cm) of ⅛" (.3cm) wide ivory satin ribbon

1¾" (4.5cm) wide ivory satin poinsettia flower with pearl center

6" (15.2cm) of 30-gauge wire

basic supplies (see page 6)

1. Bend a tip of the wire over ½" (1.3cm) and thread the other end through the bound edge of the lace. Pull the lace tightly to gather; twist the wire ends together and trim.

2. Glue the pearls to the lace circle center with a 5" (12.7cm) and a 6" (15.2cm) tail. Hold two 1½ yard (137.2cm) ribbon lengths as one and make a loopy bow with six 2" (5.1cm) loops and 6" (15.2cm) tails. Glue the bow over the pearls and the flower to the bow center. Glue the center of the remaining ribbon length to the back of the lace circle for a tie.

3. Tie one topper to the top of the cake knife and another to the server handle. For the toasting glasses, tie a topper to the top of each stem. A dot of craft glue will help keep them from slipping during the toast and will rinse away when the glasses are washed.

PICTURE FRAME

one white 8" x 10" (20.3cm x 25.4cm) mat with a 4½" x 6½" (11.4cm x 16.5cm) opening

10" x 12" (25.4cm x 30.5cm) piece of white satin fabric

10" x 12" (25.4cm x 30.5cm) piece of flat white lace

⅔ yard (61cm) of ½" (1.3cm) wide white lace with a scalloped edge

½ yard (45.7cm) of ¾" (1.9cm) wide white flower lace trim

1¼ yards (114.3cm) of 1½" (3.8cm) wide sheer white ribbon

1" (2.5cm) wide gold heart charm

9½" x 12¾" (24.1cm x 32.4cm) gold frame with an 8" x 10" (20.3cm x 25.4cm) opening

spray adhesive

basic supplies (see page 6)

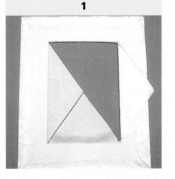

1. Spray the mat front with adhesive and cover with the satin fabric followed with the flat lace. Glue the edges of both fabrics to the back of the mat, mitering the corners (see page 7). Cut an X in the center of the fabric, cutting to 1/16" (.2cm) from the inside mat edge. Fold the flaps to the back of the mat and glue; trim as needed.

2. Glue the scalloped lace around the inside mat edge, with the scallops showing through the opening. Cut the flower trim into four 5" (12.7cm) lengths and glue to the mat front as shown. Use the ribbon to make a loopy bow with four 2" (5.1cm) loops and 12" (30.5cm) tails. Glue the bow to the upper left corner of the mat. Loop and glue the tails around the opening, and glue the charm to the bow center. Insert your engagement photo in the frame and place it on the guest book table. Use the frame later for your wedding portrait.

CANDLE DECORATION, BOUTONNIERE & CAKE KNIFE

CANDLE DECORATION

6" (15.2cm) round cream crocheted doily

3" (7.6cm) wide plastic candleholder with a center holder for a taper candle

14" (35.6cm) tall white taper candle

4" (10.2cm) of gold Zingers bullion

six mauve silk chickweed blossoms, each 1" (2.5cm) wide on a 2" (5.1cm) stem

four sprigs of white silk daisies, each 2½" (6.4cm) long with three ½" (1.3cm) wide blossoms

2⅔ yards (243.8cm) of 1" (2.5cm) wide mauve/green wire-edged ribbon

twelve 3" (7.6cm) lengths of 24-gauge wire

green floral tape

glue

BOUTONNIERE

2" (5.1cm) of gold Zingers bullion

three mauve silk chickweed blossoms, each 1" (2.5cm) wide on a 2" (5.1cm) stem

two sprigs of white silk daisies, each 2½" (6.4cm) long with three ½" (1.3cm) wide blossoms

five 3" (7.6cm) lengths of 24-gauge wire

green floral tape

CAKE KNIFE DECORATION

2" (5.1cm) of gold Zingers bullion

three mauve silk chickweed blossoms, each 1" (2.5cm) wide on a 2" (5.1cm) stem

two sprigs of white silk daisies, each 2½" (6.4cm) long with three ½" (1.3cm) wide blossoms

4" (10.2cm) wide round cream crocheted doily

⅔ yard (61cm) of ⅝" (1.6cm) wide white/gold embroidered ribbon

1" (2.5cm) brass heart charm

cotton swab, black acrylic paint, paper towels, gloss acrylic spray sealer (to antique charm)

seven 3" (7.6cm) lengths of 24-gauge wire

one 4" (10.2cm) length of 30-gauge gold wire

green floral tape

hot glue gun and sticks

For the Candle Decoration—
1. Glue the candleholder to the center of the doily. Insert the candle into holder. Make two clusters as for the boutonniere.

2. Cut the ribbon into two 1½-yard (137.2cm) lengths; use each to make a puffy bow (see page 126) with a center loop, six 2½" (6.4cm) loops and 4" (10.2cm) tails. Glue a bow into the outer area of the candleholder on each side of the candle. Glue a cluster into each bow center.

For the Boutonniere—
1. Cut bullion into two 1" (2.5cm) lengths; stretch one to 16" (40.6cm) and one to 18" (45.7cm). Form the 18" (45.7cm) length into three 2½"-3½" (6.4cm-8.9cm) loops and twist the ends around the bottom to form a stem. Repeat with the 16" (40.6cm) length, making the loops 1½"-2½" (3.8cm-6.4cm).

2. Floral tape one wire stem to each chickweed blossom and one to each daisy sprig. Hold the sprigs together at varying heights in a cluster. Place the long bullion loops behind the cluster and the short loops in front of it. Wrap the stems with floral tape to secure.

For the Cake Knife Decoration—
1. Make a cluster as for the boutonniere. Place it on the doily with the stems near the edge. Pinch the doily around the stems and secure with wire.

2. Use ribbon to make a puffy bow with a center loop, four 1½" (3.8cm) loops and 3" (7.6cm) tails. Glue it over the cluster stems.

3. Antique and seal the heart charm. Glue the charm over the cluster stem, just above the bow. Use the gold wire to attach the cluster to the cake knife.

UNITY CANDLE

UNITY CANDLE

one 3" x 6" (7.6cm x 15.2cm) white pillar candle

one wedding announcement

14" (35.6cm) of 3/8" (1cm) wide
white and green rose trim

5" x 4" (12.7cm x 10.2cm) white metal
double-ring platform candleholder with
two 2½" x 3½" (6.4cm x 8.9cm) white tall
single-ring taper candleholders

4" (10.2cm) square of floral foam for dried flowers

3 ounces (85.1g) light green plumosus

1 ounce (28.4g) white glittered German statice

½ ounce (14.2g) white baby's breath

1½ yards (137.2cm) of 5/8" (1.6cm) wide
white satin ribbon

6" (15.2cm) of 24-gauge wire

two 12" (30.5cm) white taper candles

pattern edge scissors

liquid sealer

no.6 flat brush

tacky craft glue

wax paper

two rubber bands

basic supplies (see page 6)

1. For the pillar candle, trim the announcement to 4" x 4½" (10.2cm x 11.4cm) with the pattern scissors. Use the flat brush to apply sealer to one side of the candle and let dry. Rinse the brush and apply glue to the back of the announcement, then place it over the sealed area of the candle. Roll the candle in the sheet of wax paper and secure with rubber bands to keep the announcement in place. Let dry overnight, and then glue the rose trim around the announcement ¼" (.6cm) from the edge.

2. Press the candle platform on the floral foam to make an indentation. Cut the foam to fit into the platform, and then glue to secure. Place the pillar candle on the foam and insert 2"–5" (5.1cm–12.7cm) long plumosus sprigs into the outer edge of the foam as shown. Cut the statice and baby's breath into 2"–3" (5.1cm–7.6cm) sprigs and insert among the plumosus.

3. Use 1 yard (91.4cm) of ribbon to make a loopy bow with six 2" (5.1cm) loops and 4" (10.2cm) tails. Leave 2" (5.1cm) tails on the wire used to secure the bow. Insert the bow into the foam to the right of the candle. Use the remaining ribbon to tie a shoestring bow with 1" (2.5cm) loops and 2" (5.1cm) tails around each taper candleholder as shown in the large photo. Insert the taper candles into the holders.

FLOATING CANDLE CENTERPIECE

FLOATING CANDLE CENTERPIECE

6" (15.2cm) Styrofoam wreath with a 3½" (8.9cm) wide opening

2 ounces (56.7g) green Spanish moss

seven 7" (17.8cm) long silk ivy sprigs with 1"–2" (2.5cm–5.1cm) long green leaves

two stems of white silk roses, each with three 1½" (3.8cm) wide blossoms, three ¾" (1.9cm) wide buds and many 1½" (3.8cm) long leaves

one stem of white silk double baby's breath with ten 4" (10.2cm) long stems of ¾" (1.9cm) wide flowers

2 ounces (56.7g) sprengeri

six 3½" (8.9cm) long white pearl sprays, each with three 2" (5.1cm) long stems

4¼" (10.8cm) wide clear glass bowl

2¾" (7cm) wide ivory rose floating candle

twelve to fifteen 3" (7.6cm) long floral picks with wires

six U-pins

basic supplies (see page 6)

1. Cover the wreath with moss, using U-pins to secure it. Glue six of the ivy sprigs, evenly spaced, around the outside edge of the wreath and curve them around the outside of the wreath clockwise.

2. Cut the rose blossoms and buds from the stems with 2" (5.1cm) stems. Glue, randomly spaced, around the wreath. Cut the baby's breath into 3" (7.6cm) sprigs and glue among the roses.

3. Cut the sprengeri into 2"–3" (5.1cm–7.6cm) lengths and wire three or four sprigs to a floral pick. Cut each pick to 2" (5.1cm) long, and insert them among the flowers and ivy. Cut the remaining ivy sprig into 1½" (3.8cm) long sprigs and glue to fill empty spaces. Cut the rose leaves from the stems and glue evenly among the ivy.

4. Glue the pearl sprays, evenly spaced, among the materials, extending out. Fill the bowl halfway with water and set it inside the wreath. Float the candle and light it when the reception begins.

This centerpiece is a very simple design made of inexpensive materials, so it will be easy to make many of them for your reception tables. You can give them away as gifts to friends as a thank-you for their help.

WEDDING VIDEO COVER

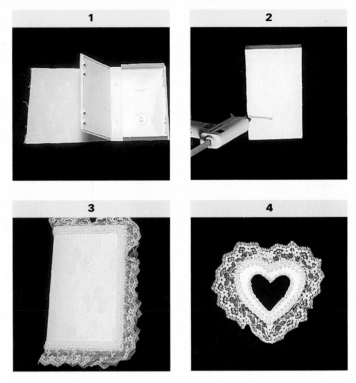

WEDDING VIDEO COVER

8" x 14" (20.3cm x 35.6cm) piece of white lace fabric

8" x 14" (20.3cm x 35.6cm) piece of white satin fabric

4³/₄" x 1¹/₈" (12.1cm x 2.9cm) white* plastic video case

1¹/₃" yards (121.9cm) of 1" (2.5cm) wide
white gathered lace

1 yard (91.4cm) of ¹/₂" (1.3cm) wide white satin gimp

4" (10.2cm) square of posterboard

⁷/₈ yard (80cm) of 4mm white fused pearls

one 7" (17.8cm) long white pearl/flower spray with
five ³/₄" (1.9cm) long pearl-centered rosebuds

tracing paper

pencil

spray glitter

basic supplies (see page 6)

*(*or spray paint the case white)*

1. Follow page 100, step 2, to adhere the lace to the satin. Open the video case and spray adhesive at an angle, taking care not to spray the edges of the cover. Close the case. Place the satin/lace right side down and place the case on it, aligning the opening edge with one 8" (20.3cm) edge of the fabric as shown. Press the fabric smoothly around the case. Cut off the excess satin/lace and set aside for step 4.

2. Use the glue gun to reinforce the spray adhesive along all edges of the fabric.

3. Beginning at the bottom back, glue lace around all edges of the cover, pinching the corners for extra fullness. Cut off the excess lace and set aside for step 4. Glue gimp over the bound edge of the lace.

4. Trace the small heart pattern from page 128. Cut one of posterboard. Cut out and discard the inner heart. Use spray adhesive to cover the front with the remaining satin/lace fabric. Cut the fabric even with the inner and outer edges. Glue lace around the outer back edge. Turn over and glue one row of pearls along the inner edge; glue two rows along the outer edge. Glue the frame to the case front as shown in the large photo above, leaving the top open to insert a photo. Bend the stem of the flower spray under and glue to the lower right. Spray with glitter.

GOLDEN BROCADE & VICTORIAN VELVET VIDEO COVERS

GOLDEN BROCADE VIDEO COVER

4³/4" x 1¹/8" (12.1cm x 2.9cm) white* plastic video case

8" x 14" (20.3cm x 35.6cm) of
beige/metallic gold brocade fabric

1¹/2 yards (137.2cm) of ³/4" (1.9cm) wide
ivory satin rickrack

1 yard (91.4cm) of 6mm ivory fused pearls

two 2" (5.1cm) long brass scroll charms

tracing paper

pencil

basic supplies (see page 6)

*(*or spray paint the case white)*

VICTORIAN VELVET VIDEO COVER

4³/4" x 1¹/8" (12.1cm x 2.9cm) white* plastic video case

8" x 14" (20.3cm x 35.6cm) of dark mauve velvet fabric

1 yard (91.4cm) of ³/4" (1.9cm) wide ivory gathered lace

⁵/8 yard (57.2cm) of 2" (5.1cm) wide
ivory crocheted flat lace with hearts

2 yards (182.9cm) of 4mm ivory fused pearls

one 4" (10.2cm) round ivory crocheted doily

1¹/8" (102.9cm) yards of ⁵/8" (1.6cm) wide mauve satin ribbon

22-gauge wire

wire cutters

one 2" (5.1cm) wide mauve/ivory silk poppy with
two 3" (7.6cm) long green leaves

basic supplies (see page 6)

*(*or spray paint the case white)*

Follow page 112, steps 1–3, to cover the case, but substitute brocade fabric for the satin/lace, omit the lace trim and substitute rickrack for the gimp. Glue pearls to the center of the rickrack. Trace the oval pattern. Cut out. Center the paper oval on the case front and lightly trace around it. Glue the remaining rickrack to the line, starting at the lower right. Leave the top open to insert a photo. Glue the charms over the rickrack ends, interlocking them as shown. Glue the remaining pearls to the center of the rickrack.

Follow page 112, steps 1–3, to cover the case, but substitute velvet fabric for the satin/lace and omit the gimp. Glue crocheted lace to the top and bottom edges with the hearts pointing inward. Glue two rows of pearls over the bound edge of the gathered lace. Glue the doily to the center front of the case. Loop the ribbon back and forth to make a bow with six 2¼" (5.7cm) loops and 6" (15.2cm) tails; wire the center and trim excess wire. Glue the bow to the doily center and knot each tail 1" (2.5cm) above the end. Glue the poppy to the bow center as shown.

GUEST BOOK COVER

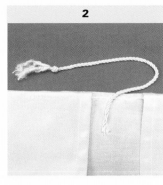

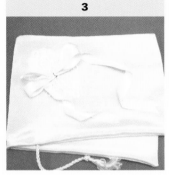

G U E S T   B O O K   C O V E R

34½" × 7½" (87.6cm × 19.1cm) piece of
ivory satin grosgrain fabric

⅓ yard (30.5cm) of ¼" (.6cm) wide ivory cord

4" × 2½" (10.2cm × 6.4cm) wide white lace appliqué

1 yard (91.4cm) of ⅞" (2.2cm) wide ivory satin ribbon

1¾" (4.5cm) wide ivory satin ribbon poinsettia flower
with pearl center

nine white 4mm flat-backed pearls

8½" × 6" (21.6cm × 15.2cm) white guest book

straight pins

fabric glue

iron

sewing machine and ivory thread

basic supplies (see page 6)

1. Lay the fabric wrong side up and fold each short edge in ⅝" (1.6cm). Sew a running stitch ½" (1.3cm) from each fold. Turn the fabric over and fold each end 7½" (19.1cm) toward the center. Pin the sides and sew ¼" (.6cm) from each side, stopping at the 7½" (19.1cm) mark, to form two pockets.

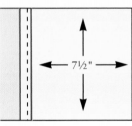

2. Turn each pocket right side out and iron flat. For the binding, fold the edge between the two pockets under ⅜" (1cm), iron and secure with fabric glue. For the bookmark, tie a knot 2" (5.1cm) from the end of the cord and fray the ends. Glue the other end 2" (5.1cm) below the top of the cover binding, just left of center.

3. *On the Front*—Glue the appliqué at an angle in the upper left corner. Use the ribbon to make a loopy bow with four 2" (5.1cm) loops, a 9" (22.9cm) tail and an 11" (27.9cm) tail. Glue the bow to the appliqué center with the shorter tail on the bottom; loop and glue the tails across the cover as shown.

4. Glue the poinsettia to the bow center; glue three pearls above the bow on the appliqué and six below. Slip the cover on the guest book.

Keep the decoration on your book cover simple because your guests will need a flat surface when writing in the book.

WEDDING PURSE

WEDDING PURSE

17½" x 9" (44.5cm x 22.9cm) of white satin fabric

⅔ yard (61cm) of 7" (17.8cm) wide white flat lace

½ yard (45.7cm) of ¾" (1.9cm) wide
white flat beading lace

½ yard (45.7cm) of 2" (5.1cm) wide
white gathered double lace

½ yard (45.7cm) of ½" (1.3cm) wide
iridescent white sequined braid

1 yard (91.4cm) of ¼" (.6cm) wide white satin ribbon

small safety pin or bodkin (for threading ribbon
through the beading trim)

one 7" (17.8cm) long white pearl spray

one 7" (17.8cm) long white pearl/flower spray with
one 2" (5.1cm) wide satin/organza rose
and a 1" (2.5cm) long rosebud

sewing machine or needle

white thread

pinking shears

wire cutters

spray glitter

basic supplies (see page 6)

1. Use pinking shears to trim ¼" (.6cm) off all edges of the satin fabric. Sew a running stitch along the center of the 7" (17.8cm) lace. Pin the stitched line ¼" (.6cm) from one long edge of the fabric, gathering to fit. Pin the beading trim over the stitching, aligning it with the fabric edge. Sew along both edges of the beading through all layers. Sew the double lace to the fabric ¼" (.6cm) from the other long edge.

2. Fold the fabric crosswise, right sides together, and pin the raw edges, matching the beading and double lace ends. Sew a ⅞" (2.2cm) seam; repeat ⅛" (.3cm) away. Use pinking shears to trim the seam close to the stitching.

3. Turn the bag right side out. Refold so the seam is centered on one side and stitch across the bottom over the previous stitching. The seam side will be the back of the bag.

4. Glue the sequined trim over the bottom seam, starting at the back seam. Thread ribbon through the beading, beginning at the back seam. Knot the ends together and trim close to the knot. Pull loops up on the center front and back to gather the purse closed. Cut the stems off the sprays. Glue the pearl spray extending downward from the front ribbon loop. Glue the pearl/flower spray over it. Spray with glitter.

Note—Dark thread was used in these photos for contrast. Use white thread.

CARD BOX

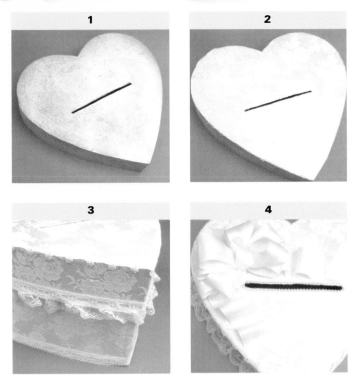

CARD BOX

8" x 14" (20.3cm x 35.6cm) heart papier-maché box

white brocade fabric pieces:
one 14" x 14" (33.6cm x 35.6cm),
one 3" x 45" (7.6cm x 114.3cm),
and one 5" x 45" (12.7cm x 114.3cm)

45" (114.3cm) of ½" (1.3cm) wide
white scalloped bridal trim

45" (114.3cm) of 2" (5.1cm) wide
white self-adhesive gathered beading lace

45" (114.3cm) of 1" (2.5cm) wide
white self-adhesive flat beading lace

25" (63.5cm) of white 4mm fused pearls

3 yards (274.3cm) of 2" (5.1cm) wide
white grosgrain ribbon

white spray paint

spray adhesive

craft knife

pencil

old newspapers

basic supplies (see page 6)

1. Set the box and lid on newspaper and paint them white inside and out; let dry. Use the craft knife to cut a 7" x ½" (17.8cm x 1.3cm) slit in the lid center.

2. Place the lid on the wrong side of the 14" (35.6cm) fabric square, trace and cut out. Spray the lid with adhesive and smooth the heart piece over it. Use the craft knife to make a slit in the center of the fabric over the card slot.

3. Spray the lid sides with adhesive, then smooth the 3" (7.6cm) fabric strip over the sides. Repeat with the 5" (12.7cm) strip even with the box bottom. Glue the fabric edges to secure. Glue bridal trim around the top edge of the lid. Glue the gathered beading lace around the lid bottom, and glue flat beading lace around the box bottom.

4. Glue the pearls around the card slot opening. Use the ribbon to make a puffy bow with a center loop, eight 3½" (8.9cm) loops and 12" (30.5cm) tails. Glue the bow to the upper left corner of the card slot and loop and glue the tails across the center of the heart.

Display the card box on the guest book table where guests can easily find it to place cards and monetary gifts. After your wedding day, move the bow to cover the card slot and use the box to keep mementos.

WEDDING TREASURE CHEST

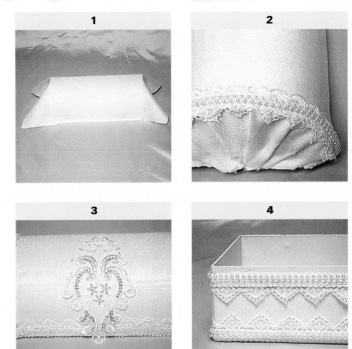

WEDDING TREASURE CHEST

one 11" x 6" x 6" (27.9cm x 15.2cm x 15.2cm)
papier maché treasure chest

½ yard (45.7cm) of 45" (114.3cm) wide
white patterned taffeta fabric

3⅝ yards (331.5cm) of ¾" (1.9cm) wide
white flat lace with one zig-zag edge

3 yards (274.3cm) of ½" (1.3cm) wide
white satin gimp braid

⅝ yard (57.2cm) of ½" (1.3cm) wide
white iridescent sequined trim

6⅛ yards (560.1cm) of 4mm
white fused pearls

one 4" x 6" (10.2cm x 15.2cm) white scroll appliqué
trimmed with rice pearls and iridescent sequins

two 7" (17.8cm) long white floral sprays,
each with five 1½" (3.8cm) wide flowers,
mini flowers and pearl sprigs

white spray paint

spray glitter

basic supplies (see page 6)

1. Spray the box and lid white; let dry. Cut a 10½" x 17" (26.7cm x 43.2cm) rectangle and a 2½" x 35" (6.4cm x 88.9cm) strip from the taffeta. Apply spray adhesive to the lid and center the fabric rectangle on it. Press to smooth in place over the curved top. Trim the front and back edges even with the lid edges.

2. Pleat the ends as shown, gluing to secure at the bottom center. Trim excess fabric even with the lid edges. Glue ¾" (1.9cm) lace along the upper curve of each end as shown. Glue gimp along each curved top edge. Glue sequined trim just inside each gimp strip, and glue two rows of pearls to the tops.

3. Glue gimp around the lower lid edge and ¾" (1.9cm) lace above it. Glue two rows of pearls to the bottom of the lace. Glue the scroll appliqué to the lid front, overlapping the trim as shown.

4. Use spray adhesive to attach the fabric strip around the box. Glue ¾" (1.9cm) lace ¼" (.6cm) below the top edge and ¼" (.6cm) above the bottom edge, points inward. Glue gimp along the top and bottom edges. Glue two rows of pearls to the lower gimp and one row to the top edge of the upper gimp. Put the lid on the box. Bend the stems of the flower sprays under and glue them to the top as shown in the large photo. Spray the entire box with glitter.

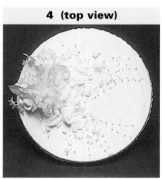

BRIDAL HATBOX

11 1/2" x 6" (29.2cm x 15.2cm) round papier-maché hatbox

1/2 yard (45.7cm) of 45" (114.3cm) wide white patterned taffeta fabric

3 yards (274.3cm) of 1/2" (1.3cm) wide white satin gimp braid

3 yards (274.3cm) of 1/2" (1.3cm) wide white iridescent sequined trim

2 yards (182.9cm) of 3/4" (1.9cm) wide white lace with one zigzag edge

four 3 1/2" x 8" (8.9cm x 20.3cm) white scroll appliqués trimmed with pearls and iridescent sequins

one white pearl spray with twelve 8" (20.3cm) long sprigs

two 7" (17.8cm) long white pearl/flower sprays, each with one 2" (5.1cm) wide satin/organza rose and a 1" (2.5cm) long rosebud

three 4" (10.2cm) wide white silk rose picks, each with one 2" (5.1cm) wide rose, five 2 1/2" (6.4cm) long leaves, a 1" (2.5cm) long bud and two 3/4" (1.9cm) wide forget-me-nots

2 1/4 yards (205.7cm) of 5/8" (1.6cm) wide white sheer ribbon with iridescent edges

gloss white spray paint

pinking shears

tacky board, spray adhesive, spray glitter

basic supplies (see page 6)

1. Spray paint the box and lid inside and out; let dry. Use pinking shears to cut a 14" (35.6cm) square and a 4 1/2" x 36" (11.4cm x 91.4cm) strip from the fabric. Spray adhesive on the top and sides of the lid. Center it on the wrong side of the 14" (35.6cm) square and press to adhere. Trim the fabric 1 1/4" (3.2cm) away and press to the lid sides, distributing the fullness evenly. Glue gimp around the edge and sequined trim above the gimp.

2. Place the 36" (91.4cm) strip wrong side up on the tacky board and spray with adhesive. Wrap the strip around the box 1/8" (.3cm) above the lower edge. Glue zigzag lace 1/4" (.6cm) above the lower edge, points upward, and 1/4" (.6cm) below the top edge, points downward.

3. Glue gimp around the top and bottom edges. Glue sequined trim inside each row of gimp. Glue the appliqués, evenly spaced, around the box sides.

4. Glue the pearl spray to the lid top 2" (5.1cm) from one edge, arranging the sprigs to fan across the top. Twist the bottom 1" (2.5cm) of the pearl/flower sprays together, bend under and glue over the pearl spray extending in a V. Glue the rose picks over the stems as shown. Use the ribbon to make a loopy bow with ten 2 1/2"–3" (6.4cm–7.6cm) loops and 3" (7.6cm) tails. Glue to the stem of the center rose pick. Spray with glitter.

HEART & PUFF SACHETS

HEART SACHET

5" (12.7cm) square of satin or taffeta fabric

5" (12.7cm) square of lace fabric

¼ cup (113.4g) potpourri

½ yard (45.7cm) of 6mm fused pearls

½ yard (45.7cm) of 1½" (3.8cm) wide gathered lace

⅔ yard (61cm) of ⅛" (.3cm) wide satin ribbon

one ½" (1.3cm) wide ribbon rose

tracing paper

pencil

basic supplies (see page 6)

(Choose colors to fit your own scheme.)

Trace and cut out the heart pattern once from satin and once from lace. Sew or glue together with a ¼" (.6cm) seam, leaving 1½" (3.8cm) open on one side. Fill with potpourri and glue the opening closed. Glue pearls over the seam. Trim any fabric that extends beyond the pearls. Glue the gathered lace around the back edge. Use the ribbon to make a loopy bow with four 1½" (3.8cm) loops and 2¼" (5.7cm) tails. Glue to the center top with the rose in the bow center. Spray lightly with glitter.

PUFF SACHET

two 12" (30.5cm) squares of posterboard

two 10½" (26.7cm) circles of lace fabric

one 10½" (26.7cm) circle of satin or taffeta fabric

½ cup (226.8g) potpourri

½ yard (45.7cm) of ⅛" (.3cm) wide satin ribbon

½ yard (45.7cm) of 3mm fused pearls

one ⅝" (1.6cm) long silk rosebud with leaves

bathroom tissue tube

four clothespins

basic supplies (see page 6)

(Choose colors to fit your own scheme.)

1. Cut a 2" (5.1cm) circle in the center of each posterboard square. Layer a lace circle, the satin circle (right side down) and the other lace circle centered over the hole; place the other posterboard square on top and secure with clothespins.

2. (A) Insert the tube 3" (7.6cm) into the hole, pushing the fabric down. Pour potpourri through the tube. Remove the tube. (B) Wrap the ribbon tightly around the fabric, below the posterboard but above the potpourri. Knot securely. Remove the sachet from the posterboard. Tie the ribbon ends in a shoestring bow with 1½" (3.8cm) loops and 2" (5.1cm) tails. Form the pearls into a loopy bow with 1½" (3.8cm) loops and 2" (5.1cm) tails. Glue over the ribbon bow with the rosebud in the bow center. Spray lightly with glitter.

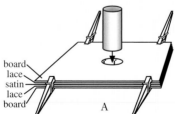

board
lace
satin
lace
board

A

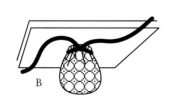

B

CHAMPAGNE GLASS FAVORS

CHERUB GLASS

one 9" (22.9cm) circle of ivory tulle net

one 9" (22.9cm) circle of white flat lace fabric

⅛ cup (56.7g) birdseed or rice

12" (30.5cm) of ⅝" (1.6cm) wide ivory satin ribbon

one 1¾" (4.5cm) long ivory plastic cherub

one 2" (5.1cm) tall clear plastic champagne glass

low-temperature glue gun and sticks,
or tacky craft glue

GLASS WITH PINK RIBBON

one 2" (5.1cm) tall clear plastic champagne glass

ten party mints

two 9" (22.9cm) circles of white tulle net with
iridescent edges

12" (30.5cm) of ¼" (.6cm) wide pink satin ribbon

one ½" (1.3cm) wide pink ribbon rose with
green leaves

low-temperature glue gun and sticks,
or tacky craft glue

Lay the ivory tulle over the lace, place the seed or rice in the center and gather the lace and tulle around the filler. Wrap the ribbon around the bundle above the filler and tie in a shoestring bow with 1¼" (3.2cm) loops and 1¼" (3.2cm) tails. Glue the cherub diagonally to the bow center. Place the bundle in the glass.

Fill the glass with candy. Lay both tulle circles over the top of the glass and gather them under the bowl. Wrap with the ribbon to secure, making a shoestring bow with loops and 1" (2.5cm) tails. Glue the rose to the bow center.

RING BEARER PILLOW

R I N G   B E A R E R
P I L L O W

2½ yards (228.6cm) of 4" (10.2cm) wide
ivory gathered lace

two 8" (20.3cm) square pieces of
ivory satin grosgrain fabric

9" (22.9cm) of ⅝" (1.6cm) wide ivory satin ribbon

4 ounces (113.4g) polyester fiberfill

1 yard (91.4cm) of 4mm ivory fused pearls

4" x 2¾" (10.2cm x 7cm) white lace appliqué

⅓ yard (30.5cm) of ⅛" (.3cm) wide ivory satin ribbon

twenty-four 4mm white flat-backed pearls

fabric glue

needle with large eye

straight pins

sewing machine

ivory thread

basic supplies (see page 6)

1. Use the needle and thread to sew a running stitch through the bound edge of the lace. Pull to gather until it is half its length. Lay a fabric square right side up and pin the gathered lace edge around its edge. Sew a running stitch ⅛" (.3cm) in from the fabric and lace edges, leaving 2" (5.1cm) open.

2. For the handle, lay the remaining fabric square right side up. Lay the ⅝" (1.6cm) ribbon across the center of the square and pin its edges. Sew each ribbon end ⅛" (.3cm) from each fabric edge; trim any excess. Place the fabric squares right sides together (so the lace and ribbon are sandwiched in between) and pin. Sew a running stitch ¼" (.6cm) from the fabric edge, leaving a 4" (10.2cm) opening at one side.

3. Remove the pins and turn the pillow right side out. Stuff with fiberfill and sew the opening closed. Glue the fused pearls around the edge between the fabric and lace on the pillow front. Glue the appliqué to the pillow center.

4. Thread the needle with the ⅛" (.3cm) ribbon and make a single stitch in the appliqué center. Tie a shoestring bow with 2" (5.1cm) loops and 2½" (6.4cm) tails. Glue ten flat-backed pearls to the appliqué and the remaining flat-backed pearls to the pillow in rows as shown.

Tie the wedding rings to the pillow with a shoestring bow. If you are worried about the rings getting lost, use gold metal rings from the craft store for the same effect.

Note—Red thread was used to make the stitches visible in the photo: Use ivory thread.

FLOWER BASKET

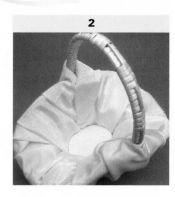

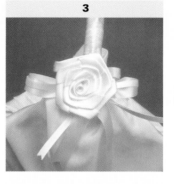

F L O W E R   B A S K E T

9" x 6" x 6½" (22.9cm x 15.2cm x 16.5cm) basket
with a 4½" (11.4cm) tall handle

one 4" (10.2cm) square of posterboard

white grosgrain fabric: one 28" (71.1cm) square,
and one 5" (12.7cm) square

4⅓ yards (396.2cm) of ⅝" (1.6cm) wide
white satin ribbon

1⅓ yards (121.9cm) of ¼" (.6cm) wide
white satin ribbon

three 2½" (6.4cm) wide white satin ribbon roses

basic supplies (see page 6)

1. Trace the basket bottom on the posterboard; cut out slightly smaller and set aside for step 2. Place the basket on the center of the wrong side of the 28" (71.1cm) fabric square. Fold the fabric edges up and over the basket rim to make pleats. Glue the front and back fabric edges into the basket bottom.

2. Fold the side fabric edges inside the basket, going around the handles. Fold the raw edges in and glue to make a seam down each inner side. Cover the posterboard circle with the 5" (12.7cm) fabric square and glue the edges to the back. Glue the circle in the basket bottom.

3. Pull any loose fabric around the handle base up to and around the handle. Wrap the ⅝" (1.6cm) ribbon around the handle, starting over the loose fabric. Finish wrapping the handle by binding the loose fabric on the other handle base. Hold 24" (61cm) of the ⅝" (1.6cm) and the ¼" (.6cm) ribbon together and tie a shoestring bow with 2½" (6.4cm) loops and 6" (15.2cm) tails around a handle base. Trim the tails to 4"–6" (10.2cm–15.2cm) and glue a rose to the bow center. Repeat for the other side.

4. Use the remaining ⅝" (1.6cm) ribbon to make a puffy bow with ten 2" (5.1cm) loops and one 14" (35.6cm) tail. Glue the bow to the basket front 1½" (3.8cm) above the bottom. Wrap the tail around the basket and glue behind the bow. Glue the remaining ribbon rose to the bow center.

Fill the basket with fresh or dried rose petals to be scattered by a child.

SHOESTRING & COLLAR BOWS

S H O E S T R I N G   B O W

C O L L A R   B O W

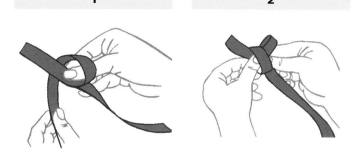

1   **2**

1. Measure the desired tail length from the end of the ribbon and make a loop of the specified length. Wrap the free end of the ribbon loosely around the center of the bow.

2. Form a loop in the free end of the ribbon and push it through the center loop. Pull the loops in opposite directions to tighten, then pull on the tails to adjust the size of the loops. Trim each tail diagonally or in an inverted V.

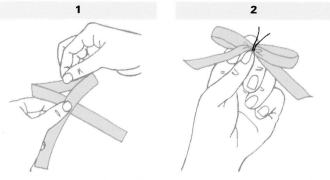

1   **2**

1. Form a ribbon length into a circle, crossing the ends in front. Pinch together, forming a bow, and adjust the loop size and tail length. If no tails are desired, form the length into a circle and just barely overlap the ends before pinching into a bow.

2. Wrap the center with wire and twist tightly at the back to secure. Trim the wire ends, wrap a short length of ribbon over the center wire and glue the ends at the back. Cut each tail diagonally or in an inverted V.

LOOPY BOW

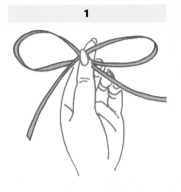

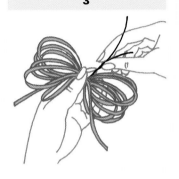

1. Measure the desired tail length from the end of the ribbon and make a loop on each side of your thumb. If a center loop is needed, measure the desired tail length from the end of the ribbon and make the center loop before the bow loops.

2. Continue making loops on each side of your thumb until the desired number is reached (for a ten-loop bow, make five loops on each side).

3. Wrap the center with wire and twist tightly at the back to secure. If a center loop was made, insert the wire through it before twisting the ends at the back. Trim the wire ends. Cut each tail diagonally. If a second set of tails is desired, secure the bow by wrapping a length of ribbon around the center and tying it at the back.

L O O P Y   B O W

#2 loopy bow with a center loop

#3 loopy bow with extra tails

FLAT BOW

F L A T   B O W

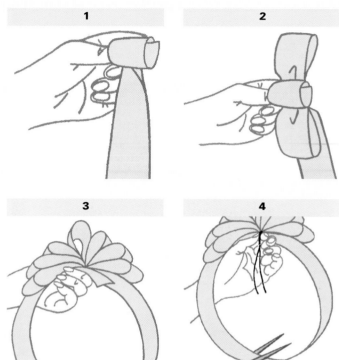

1. Begin with one end of the ribbon and make a center loop of the desired length. Twist the ribbon to keep the right side showing.

2. Make a loop of the specified length on one side of your thumb. Twist the ribbon and form a matching loop on the other side.

3. Continue making loops of graduating sizes on each side of your thumb, positioning each just under the last, until the desired number is reached. For tails: Bring the ribbon end up and hold it under the bow.

4. Insert a wire length through the center loop. Bring the ends to the back, catching the ribbon end, and twist to secure. Cut the ribbon tails to the desired lengths, then trim each tail diagonally or in an inverted V.

OBLONG BOW

O B L O N G   B O W

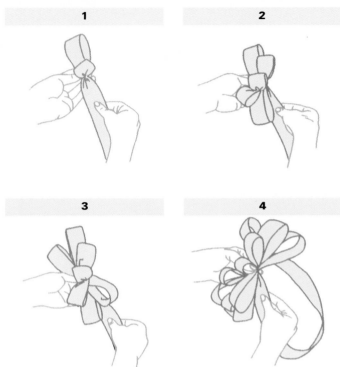

1. Form a center loop by wrapping the ribbon around your thumb. Twist the ribbon a half turn to keep the right side showing, and then make a loop on one side of the center loop.

2. Make another half twist and another loop on the other side. Make another half twist and form a slightly longer loop on each side of your hand; notice these loops are placed diagonally to the first loops.

3. Make two more twists and loops on the opposite diagonal. Continue for the desired number of loops, making each set slightly longer than the previous set. For tails: Bring the ribbon end up and hold in place under the bow.

4. Insert a wire through the center loop, bring the ends to the back of the bow and twist tightly to secure. Trim each tail diagonally or in an inverted V.

PUFFY BOW

P U F F Y   B O W

1. If a center loop is required, begin with one end of the ribbon length and make the center loop. Twist the ribbon to keep the right side showing. If no center loop is called for, begin with step 2.

2. Make a loop on one side of your thumb. Give the ribbon a twist and make another loop, the same length as the first, on the other side of your thumb. Continue making loops and twists until the desired number is reached (a ten-loop bow has five loops on each side), ending with a twist. For tails: Bring the ribbon end up and hold in place under the bow, making a long loop (two or more loops can be made for multiple tails).

3. Insert a wire through the center loop, bring the ends to the back of the bow and twist tightly to secure. Trim each tail diagonally or in an inverted V.

Patterns

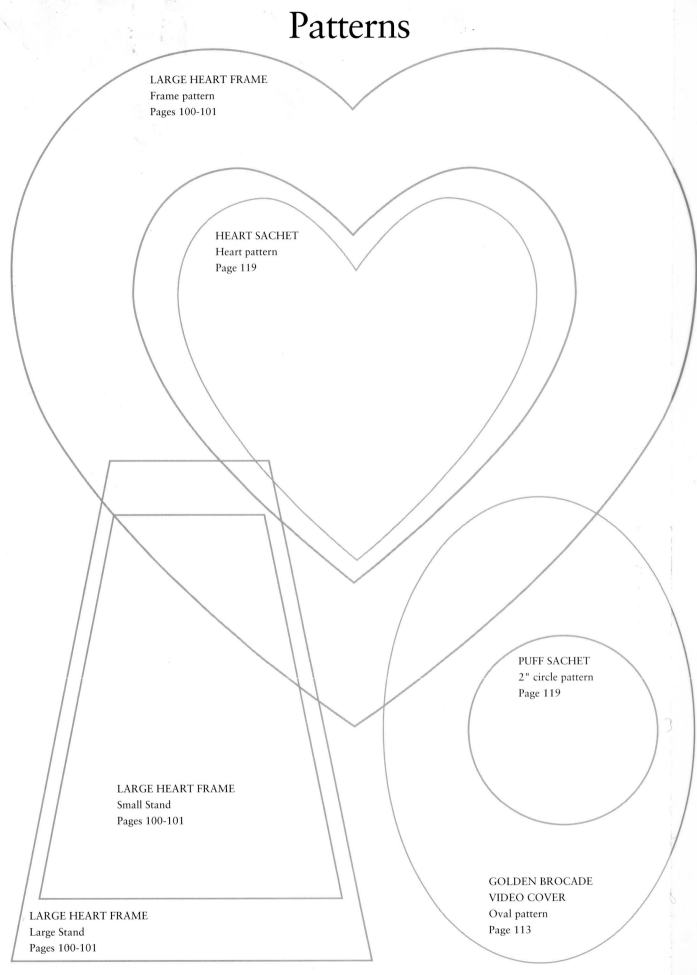

LARGE HEART FRAME
Frame pattern
Pages 100-101

HEART SACHET
Heart pattern
Page 119

PUFF SACHET
2" circle pattern
Page 119

LARGE HEART FRAME
Small Stand
Pages 100-101

GOLDEN BROCADE
VIDEO COVER
Oval pattern
Page 113

LARGE HEART FRAME
Large Stand
Pages 100-101